ALL TOGETHER

ALL TOGETHER

✦

The Formidable Journey to the Gold with the 1964 Olympic Crew

William A. Stowe

iUniverse, Inc.
New York Lincoln Shanghai

ALL TOGETHER
The Formidable Journey to the Gold with the 1964 Olympic Crew

iUniverse books may be ordered through booksellers or by contacting:

iUniverse
2021 Pine Lake Road, Suite 100
Lincoln, NE 68512
www.iuniverse.com
1-800-Authors (1-800-288-4677)

ISBN: 0-595-34388-0

Printed in the United States of America

ALL TOGETHER dedicated to the memory of my Kent School Coach Tote Walker and his wife Elise, who for years encouraged me in rowing and writing.

Contents

Acknowledgements

Thanks to all those who are named and quoted in this true rowing story. Without their willingness to express themselves frankly, this book could not be a true accounting of the accomplishment. The book is a group effort and their interviews are reported with accuracy. Thanks to Emory Clark, our mighty five man who allowed me to quote from his well written Lucy's Log. Inspiration for this collected effort must go to Tote and Elise Walker, who for years before their deaths, urged me to write this accounting of the 1964 Olympic Games. Special thanks is extended to Walter Buckley, a fraternity brother at Cornell, who called me out of the blue and suggested, encouraged, and supported such an effort. Without him I would not have had the audacity to begin.

Bill Wallace, a longtime friend and retired New York TIMES sportswriter performed the final edit, after I had received some sincere help from Harvard oarsmen and authors Robert Whitney and Eric Sigward. As a total novice to the art of writing and without any previous knowledge of the publishing business, my thanks to the many friends and acquaintances who have shown an interest in this project and attempted to assist me.

Finally, special thanks to my loving wife Barbara, whose knowledge of our language and use of the word processor, coupled with great encouragement, pushed me to completion of ALL TOGETHER.

Introduction—All Together

Before issuing a command in an eight-oared rowing shell, the coxswain will gather the attention of each individual oarsman by saying—shouting—"All together", and then give his directions, be it to start a workout by lifting the boat off the boathouse rack or later, at the end of the row, to lift the boat out of the water from the dock—and whatever need be done in between to facilitate a team movement of this crew. For example, the coxswain might collect his oarsmen's diverted minds toward his goal to get the boat going by saying, "All together now. Ready…Row." The translation? Forget your individual thoughts. Put them toward moving the shell in unity—as one.

This saying "All Together" was adopted as the motto of the Vesper Boat Club sometime soon after its founding on February 22, 1865, and it is incorporated in the Club shield. The club name of Vesper represents that time of the evening reserved for quiet reflection and prayer. Rowers know that time spent on the water is special, reverent—almost sacred.

During a time when I was rowing in Philadelphia, I missed church some Sundays because of a workout. My minister, who had a rowing background at Cornell University, said that perhaps I was closer to God out there on the Schuylkill River than I could ever be in his building of worship.

The Vesper Boat Club embraced that spirit. To gain order from the individual chaos of life, the coxswain merely had to say "All Together." And the oarsmen melted into one force with a purpose and direction.

The collection of individuals that came together to compete for a place on the United States 1964 Olympic team could hardly have been more diverse or unstereotyped. A rag tag outfit at best we only had one purpose in common, that of rowing and winning—overcoming everything we came up against. In spite of unthinkable differences in backgrounds, interests and personality, this collection of characters could come together as one, with astonishing strength and precision. All it took was the command "All Together."

What follows is the saga of this quest which resulted in an American victory at the Olympic Games, the sport's premier event. This was accomplished in Japan in 1964 by the eight from Philadelphia's Vesper Boat Club that made up a bit of history not replicated for forty years. I was fortunate, and am proud, to have been a part of that effort which buried individual identity and differences. "All Together."

Preface—A Few Rowing Terms

When I set out to write this book it was my hope that along the way I might educate neophytes of rowing through some of the sport's fascinating points. By weaving a few technical issues into the story, I can painlessly expand the reader's knowledge of rowing. But first there are basic elements that must be understood before proceeding.

Those that follow college or high school rowing refer to the sport as "crew"—a good term when speaking of four or eight-oared rowing. One should never use the redundant "crew team," a mistake common to uninitiated newspaper and magazine writers and editors.

Let's examine the overall picture. Rowing is divided into two distinct classifications, the first the more common sweep rowing in which each participant wields a single oar that assists in moving the boat—also known as the shell—through the water. Sweep boats include the most common eight-oared shell, consisting of eight oars being pulled by eight individuals—four on each side, port and starboard, with a coxswain in the stern to steer.

The four additional sweep boats include the four-with-coxswain and the pair-with-coxswain; plus the four and pair without the coxswain, also known as a straight four or pair.

Steering in a coxswainless boat is generally accomplished by either the bowman or the stroke. One foot is attached to a cable that leads to the rudder. Because most race courses are straight, only a slight twist of the foot is sufficient to alter the boat's course.

The oars for sweep rowing are called oars, or blades, and are just over twelve feet long.

The other classification is sculling. While sweep oarsmen handle one oar, a sculler grasps an oar with each hand. The distinction between the two perhaps is as radical as a comparison to the distinction between tennis and ping-pong.

The sculling oar is nine to ten feet long and can rightfully be called a scull. Any rowing boat can be called a shell. Sometimes a single shell is inappropriately called a scull when it should be referred to as a sculling shell.

A single sculling shell is rowed by one person, the double by two and the quadruple by four. There are competitive events for all three.

Two sweep oarsmen are always called a pair while two scullers are a double. Four sweep oarsmen make up a four, and four scullers a quad as in quadruple. Got it?

Scholastic and collegiate rowing generally consists of sweep rowing in eights and fours because it is easier to learn with one oar than two and one coach can instruct more athletes in the same time frame.

As for coxswains they come small and light so the rowers do not have to lug around too much weight that is producing no speed. Rowing rules maintain that a coxswain must weigh at least 50 kilos (112 pounds) or else the boat is required to carry sand bags to bring the weight to that minimum. Anything over the 50 kilos is boat-slowing baggage.

Speaking with a coxswain you will sometimes be led to believe that he or a she is the most important and indispensable person in the boat. That might be true with beginner rowers when the coxswain may teach the proper technique of blade (oar) work. The coxswain also is the eyes of the boat and is supposed to avoid collisions and keep the shell on a straight course in the middle of the assigned racing lane.

The coxswain will also tell the rowers where they are and what position they are in during the course of a race, eliminating the need for them to be distracted from their job of pulling.

But as the rowers gain experience the job of the coxswain becomes less essential, and also one subject to blame by others in the crew. Poor steering by the cox can be an easy excuse for losing a race while oarsmen, following a victory, rarely credit good steering.

Did I say oarsmen? I will attempt to give gender equity in this writing but remember that I do come from the era when rowing was done only by men and in Olympic competition only by heavyweight men.

It is not with malice that I might refer to oarsmen when I mean anyone that who pulls an oar. Rowing has prospered with the inclusion of both the women rowers and the lightweight classifications, meaning male crews averaging 155 pounds or less and women lightweights less. Of course in international races the pounds turn to kilos of various amounts.

There was considerable debate when the National Association of Amateur Oarsmen (NAAO) changed its name to the United States Rowing Association (USRA). The NAAO had the distinction of being the oldest athletic governing body in America. But the women won the day and "Oarsmen" was stricken from the title. Perhaps this change was timely because the pure amateur has all but disappeared at the highest levels of competitive rowing.

To a novice one of the most interesting aspects of competitive rowing is the use of the sliding seat, making it possible for the rowers to use their legs to the fullest extent. While the feet are stationary and laced shoes fastened to the boat, the seat is on small wheels and travels about thirty inches forward and back. This range allows the athlete to power the boat with his legs, these being the strongest of the three components of the drive with the oar—the arms, the back, and the legs.

The sliding seat with wheels was introduced around the turn of the 20th century. Prior to that the oarsmen sat in leather padded pants sliding forward and back on a greased surface.

Being a sport on the water, rowing utilizes many nautical terms. The bow of the shell is the first part of the boat, the tip in the direction it is heading. The stern is the back end of the boat, and generally the location of the rudder, which steers the boat.

There are two sides to a boat, nautically labeled port or starboard, or left and right. This distinction has often given rowers fits because they come to specialize in rowing on one side or the other. You are known as a port or starboard rower.

I rowed port which meant that as I sat in the boat my oar went out to right of my body. But since I was sitting backwards in the shell my oar was really on the left, or port, side of the boat. Think about it.

Even after three years an officer in the United States Navy, I still have to stop and think of the location of my oar in relation to the boat before I can determine which is port or starboard while out sailing.

The position of the oarsmen in a boat also gives some confusion. The bowman is the one sitting closest to the front end of the boat. He is also labeled number one, or #1. The numbers increase seat by seat toward the stern, with the last oarsman being # 8, also known as the stroke. Just to confuse matters, the Europeans number the boat in reverse, with the stroke being the #1 man and the bow #8.

The stroke is the pace setter of the racing machine and he determines when to sprint or when to vary the cadence of the crew's rhythm. The additional rowers in the boat must follow the lead of the stroke, whose oar they can easily see without turning their heads. Perhaps the stroke compares to the quarterback in football.

The placement of oarsmen in the shell is important, and the middle four, that is numbers three through six, are commonly called the "engine room" since they are likely to be the largest and strongest ones in the boat.

The lighter bow pair generally possess a skilled touch since much of the delicate balance of the shell rests with their blade work. The seven man, the one sitting directly behind the stroke, is critical in following the exact movement of the stroke for a smooth maintenance of the cadence.

At the Olympic games in 1964 there were seven different rowing events raced in order, the four with coxswain, the pair without, the single sculls, the four without coxswain, the pair with coxswain, the double sculls, and the eight.

The contemporary Olympic program is quite different due to the inclusion of women's and lightweight rowing. Gone are two men's heavyweight events, the pair and four with coxswains. All Olympic boats race a standard course of 2,000 meters, just over a mile and a quarter.

About the time America lost its domination of international rowing, in the 1960's, the rigging of the racing equipment got more technical.

The introduction of plastics and carbon fiber revolutionized equipment. The providers experimented with design changes and now there are dozens of minute opportunities to fine tune a racing shell, making it faster—or messing it all up.

The fiber glass and carbon fiber boats are far faster and lighter today than the wooden boats of 50 years ago and more. The standards for racing are higher, the racing times ever lower. How much is in the equipment and how much is in the men—and women—is continuously disputed.

1

The Story

The story of the 1964 Vesper Boat Club eight that went on to become the surprise Olympic champion is a narrative accounting of nine men who came together and achieved the highest pinnacle possible in the sport of rowing. It is not the personal story of Bill Stowe, even though I am the one offering the accounting. Rather the Vesper story is one of differing individuals who were brought together in a rather bizarre manner to assist in achieving their individual dreams, ones that could only be realized through the actions of the whole. Indeed this crew turned out to be far more that the sum of all its diverse parts.

Perhaps a preferable story would be one where the ending remains a mystery through all the early pages. Is suspense preferable to knowing the outcome? Did we win, or didn't we win? But you read this tale knowing the outcome just as you might read an account of World War II aware of who won. It is the battles that hold your interest and it is my intention that the suspense will come from learning how the nearly impossible was achieved.

And then at the end what else did each of us believe we won, besides that gold medal, 40 years later?

The goal of winning gold was not the incentive that brought us together in the first place. In my case I blundered into Vesper and the Olympic Games. I had enjoyed rowing and was able to excel at the sport, liking the challenge of winning a seat in a good boat. I personally knew little of the Olympic Games, or of the rowing therein.

Four years before I might have had a chance to reach the Olympics at Rome as the stroke of a very good Cornell crew. But a fraternity sophomoric prank cost me my collegiate eligibility that season. Someone suggested that I could best start this story by expressing my personal burning desire to achieve Olympic greatness, to make up for my blunder of 1960. Such was not the case.

Others had different reasons for the quest. Several were out to prove that they were better oarsmen than their college experience had shown. The two brothers in the boat were intent, or content, to become national champions rather than global champions.

In today's media accounts of successful athletes we often hear about childhood dreams and goals of Olympic gold that go back as early as the ages of five. Swimmers and skaters seem to recall first strokes and steps with the Olympics as the ultimate end. But in 1964 the Olympic Games were truly amateur and did not have the glitter and publicity that today's more commercial games portray.

It was less than a big deal. A serious Olympic effort never occurred to me until I was asked to join Vesper by Jack Kelly. As I was naive to the process, becoming a medal contender was beyond my wildest dreams. So I came to realize the greatness of the achievement as it transpired. And reflecting upon it over forty years makes the story even more incredible. The victory was neither the result of one or two vital ingredients nor one or two key characters, but rather a recipe of over one hundred critical factors that culminated in the Vesper boat being the best in the world. There are no stars in rowing—no ace quarterback or star pitcher—but a collective effort that comes together to create a magnificent performance.

When and where did the 1964 Olympic victory start?

I have always believed the competitiveness of the Vesper crew had deep roots in the club's history. It was founded in February, 1865, as the Washington Boat Club on the west bank of the Schuylkill River in the heart of Philadelphia and the current boathouse stands on the original site. There's a cornerstone dated 1865. The first boathouse was constructed in combination with neighboring Malta Boat Club at 10 East River Drive—which was renamed 120 years later as Kelly Drive.

Nineteenth century construction was carried out by those members of the club who were tradesmen, and local building materials were used. The Victorian architecture is typical of the period.

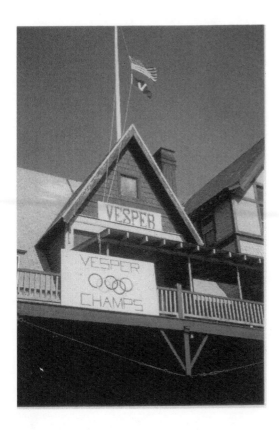

But the Washington Boat Club went bankrupt before attaining any notoriety. Reestablished on New Years Day of 1870 as the Vesper Boat Club, the organization's stated purpose was racing, not society. No dances.

Vesper flourished. An example of its success came on July 21, 1900 when its eight won the national championship race of the National Association of Amateur Oarsmen's regatta on the Harlem River in New York, thus gaining the right to represent the United States for the first rowing competition of the modern Olympic games.

There was concern about finding enough money to send the eight to Paris, the site of the second of the modern Olympics, and the club had to come up with $1,000 to make the trip. Since the N.A.A.O. did not fill the grandstand for its regatta nationals there was a shortage of cash. A thousand dollars was a lot of money in 1900. Also the Olympics were an unknown commodity lacking popular appeal. But the club raised the funds and on August 1 the Olympic eight with coxswain headed for Paris from New York aboard the S.S. Westerland. Because money was so tight the contingent went without a spare oarsman, Vesper taking the chance no one would become ill.

By August 16th the Vespers had arrived in Paris and had their first practice in a borrowed shell, their own delayed on the Cherbourg-to-Paris railroad trip. According to the Vesper Boat Club Centennial Celebration program, the coach, Pat Dempsey, had announced his men "were in fine health but were 'hog fat' from the pounds put on during the ocean crossing."

The Olympics in 1900 were nothing close to the current slick productions. The events were held over a five month period, poorly publicized and poorly attended. In spite of the shabby organization and planning, the games attracted 1,330 athletes from 22 nations. The program had been expanded to include new sports like rowing and for the first time in ancient or modern history, women were invited to participate—but only in golf and lawn tennis. Seventy six years later women would row in the Olympics.

The rowing events were held on the Courbevoie course over the fast-moving Seine River in the shadow of the newly erected Eiffel Tower. To quote again from the Vesper Boat Club's Centennial Celebration program, "The race course on the Seine was the same distance as when the Vespers raced and won on the Harlem River: 1 mile and 153 yards. On August 25th, the Dutch crew won the first heat of the games in 4 minutes and 49 3/5s seconds. Vesper easily won the second heat with a time of 5 minutes and 15 2/5s seconds, defeating France by fifteen lengths. Coach Dempsey explained that a stiff wind across the Seine barred Vesper from a faster finish."

One might hope that it was good sportsmanship that kept the Americans from disheartening the poor French by winning by more.

At 5:15 on the evening of the 26th of August, several thousand spectators lined the banks of the Seine at Asniers, with many Americans among them. According to the Vesper historian, "It was thought that the Americans would win, and the bookmakers flatly refused all bets. The Belgian crew was second choice at 3 to 1.

"Joining Vesper were the Minerva Eight from Amsterdam, the German eight of Hamburg and the Ghent crew from Belgium. The Vespers assumed the lead after a dozen strokes, and held their advantage for a half mile. Then the Belgian crew at a stroke rate of 38 passed the Amsterdam crew and began to challenge Vesper for the lead. Brussels took second position and as its shell challenged the American boat, Vesper responded to cheers from the crowd and dug into the water faster with a determination so that clear water separated the leaders. The

Vespers increased their distance during the race and finished four open lengths ahead, their stroke-rate steady and never exceeding 34 strokes per minute."

So Vesper was the first American crew to win an Olympic championship. To quote the club historian, "The newspapers remarked on differences in European and American styles, taking special notice of how the American's long, clean and beautiful style contrasted the German's decidedly short stroke, which brought them a dead last. American newspapers touted that every man on the winning crew was 'trained to the hour and in the best of condition, which speak volumes for the American method of preparation.' Americans were physically superior to their opponents, their big frames and athletic build evoking compliments when they carried their oars from the boathouse."

Sixty four years later, at Tokyo, the Germans again fell victim to their shorter stroke, designed to maximize tailwind conditions which failed to materialize.

Vesper again qualified to represent the United States in the 1904 Games, held in St. Louis, but the sport was termed merely an exhibition due to lack of sufficient entries. Vesper "won" over a Canadian eight and no medals were given out.

In 1905 Vesper took a trip to England to compete in the illustrious Henley Royal Regatta and the crew did not do well, falling short of expectations. Perhaps those young Americans did not quite comprehend the pomp and circumstance of the English. They behaved badly too and as a result the club was banned from future admission to the regatta. This ban was to play an interesting role in the middle of the 20th century.

Each oarsman had been given $100 in spending money for the ocean trip home. This was a breach of amateur rules in an era of strict sporting codes and would later cloud the amateur standing of the Vesper Boat Club.

After these first two Olympic games, eights from the United States did not win medals at the games of 1906 (Athens), 1908 (London) or 1912 (Stockholm). Following World War I college crews took over the American representation in international events and did so with great success, winning every Olympic eight-oared championship from 1920 through 1956.

2

John B. Kelly Senior

In 1909 an 18-year old novice rower named John B. Kelly joined the Vesper Boat Club. As the ensuing decade unfolded this nobody became Vesper's and America's greatest oarsman—upon a comely river already made famous by anonymous rowing roustabouts and an eminent painter of their images, Thomas Eakins.

According to his son Jack, "My father rowed in various types of boats for a few years, but finally settled down to single and double sculling. He became the Philadelphia champion and almost won the American title before World War I. In 1919, he won his first of two United States titles, the second the next year.

"Following the war, the Olympics were revived in Antwerp and for the 1920 Games my father qualified to represent the United States in both the single and the double. In the latter event, he paired with his cousin, Paul Costello. I don't believe my father's success in winning both these events in the Olympiad has ever been duplicated."

They have not.

Earlier in 1920 John B. Kelly had sought to compete in Britain's esteemed Henley Royal Regatta, but his entry was refused by the stewards. True to English tradition, they did not elaborate on the reasons.

Rumor still prevails that the rejection came because he was a bricklayer and the English gentry would not allow a common tradesman, who worked with his hands, to despoil the regatta of gentlemen.

The jingoistic American press picked up on this incident and the rumor—for that's all it was—became a chapter in American rowing lore.

Jack Kelly Jr. years later said, "While it's a wonderful and believable story, it simply is not true. The entry's rejection was prompted by the boorish behavior of Vesper oarsmen and the subsequent Vesper ban from the regatta dating back to 1905."

A generation afterward the regatta ban was lifted and the Vesper entry of John B. Kelly Jr. was accepted. So Jack, in 1946 rowed his single at the Henley

Regatta. In 1947 he won the Diamond Sculls on the Thames at Henley, the most renowned race for single scullers the world over. As the press put it Jack avenged his father's snobbish rejection in 1920.

According to Jack Kelly Jr., "Up until 1922, Vesper was probably the most successful rowing club in the United States, a fact to which the great number of old trophies on its walls will attest. But in that year internal strife occurred, and my father and many of his friends left Vesper and organized the Penn Athletic Club."

From that club Kelly Senior went on the win the 1924 Olympic double sculls gold medal at Paris. Two years later he retired from competition and, his son related, "He began to take on the role of a sponsor and part-time coach. Vesper in the meantime had slipped into comparative oblivion."

Kelly Senior was a dashing handsome man, as intense in his contracting business as he was his in rowing. He was also intense in his social life and gossip hinted his departure from Vesper was caused by a discovered romantic tryst with the wife of one of Vesper's officers.

More to the point, this Philadelphia "bricklayer" was in the process of creating a huge construction empire. It did not hurt that Kelly was aligned with the Democratic Party, and his ties with President Franklin D. Roosevelt during the New Deal years increased his prestige and wealth. The evidence is in the many Federal buildings of the late 1930's made of Kelly's red brick.

Being Irish Catholic in established Philadelphia circles was hardly an asset in the era of John B. Kelly, and he was not exactly embraced by old families of the Main Line and Chestnut Hill. The good looks, newly earned wealth and beautiful family—one which would in time include daughter Grace, the future movie star and princess—could not bend old guard attitudes.

Young Jack Kelly at the dedication of the statue of his father, John B. Kelly, along the Schuylkill River in Philadelphia.

Kelly was unfazed. He announced his Democratic candidacy to be mayor of Philadelphia on the steps of the Republican stronghold, the Union League Club. He lost the election but not the admiration of the minorities in the City of Brotherly Love, which helped in business dealings and union transactions.

Kelly wanted the best for son Jack, and when the dust was settling from World War II he more or less bought the Vesper Boat Club. He had introduced his son to the sport around the age of nine, Jack helping to steer Penn A.C. crews from the coxswain's seat, or rowing himself in a practice boat. Sometimes father and son would row together in a double.

By 1944, 17 year old Jack was training seriously under the direction of his father at Penn A.C., where political battles within the club never abated. So when the Vesper president and family friend, Dr. Charles W. Riggall, suggested a Kelly return to Vesper it was accepted. Immediately Jack became Vesper's only competitive oarsman.

Twenty years later, when the Vesper Olympic boat was assembled, Doc Riggall was still president.

"In 1944, the Vesper Boat House at 10 Boathouse Row was in a bad state of disrepair," Jack Kelly recalled. "It had only two or three singles in rowable condition. Even though Doc Riggall had done his best to keep the club from expiring, the membership consisted of about six men, all over competitive ages. A restoration program was started immediately.

"To get active oarsmen Vesper began sponsorship of high school rowing. That was quite successful and in 1945 Vesper boated its first crews in 20 years."

From LaSalle High School came a youth named Bill Knecht who in time would be the first member of our 1964 Olympic eight.

Also from LaSalle came Joe Toland who has recalled his early Vesper days. "Mr. Kelly was a wonderful man to the LaSalle kids. Every day after practice he had milk, sandwiches, and cookies catered for the rowers. For poor kids from the East Falls area of Philadelphia, this was heavenly treatment.

"He was a huge man and a hero to us. In 1939 our scroungy group of eleven neighborhood kids were going door to door selling raffle chances so we could buy uniforms for our newly established pee-wee football team. Mr. Kelly reached into his pocket and outfitted the whole group. And not with cheap cotton jerseys, but the best. He continued to be great to us for the rest of his life."

Mr. Kelly died in June,1960. Allen Rosenberg, then an anonymous coxswain absorbing everything around Vesper, has this recall: "Mr. Kelly's presence in the boathouse was always memorable. He wore the finest clothes, all hand-tailored, and perfectly fitted over his athletic and handsome figure. He was an inspiration for success and wealth. While he stayed in the shadows and spoke in a monotone, we all knew he was strongly in charge."

Harry Parker, a rowing icon, was a Vesper sculler in his youth and thus a contemporary of Jack Kelly—whose nickname among fellow oarsmen was Kell.

Parker tells this story: "I got an invitation to go and meet Kell's old man before going to race in the 1960 Henley Regatta. He was a classic man. Didn't have much to say, but gave me a hundred dollar bill to help with my expenses. I had never even seen a hundred dollar bill. I was both appreciative and impressed. I remember taking some ribbing about wearing a Kelly-for-Brickwork tee shirt while training on the Thames River. But I was grateful for his support."

Rosenberg became our Vesper 1964 coach. And Parker, at Harvard, the most successful college crew coach in history by any measure.

The unrelenting side to this Mr. Kelly, the formidable Irish gentleman backing the quiet Vesper club, was a fierce, competitiveness which, as I reflect, set the tone that sustained through the sixties and all the way to Tokyo.

Joe Toland has said it best. "Mr. Kelly wanted winners. Not a stable of losers. And being a nice guy wasn't good enough for him. He would only support those who tried their hardest and won."

Toland recalls racing in the Vesper eight at Buffalo in 1949, en route to the Canadian Henley Regatta at St. Catherine's, Ontario. And losing there by a tenth of a second.

"The crew was commiserating after the race and was wondering about the future of the boat. We noticed the club big-shots nearby and I was selected to ask Mr. Kelly what to do—to pack the boats for St. Catherine's. Or for home?"

So the brave brash Toland asked, "Are we going to ship these boats from here to St. Catherine's? Or are we going to put them on the trailer back to Philadelphia?"

John B. Kelly Senior replied, "They are going home. Anybody that loses a boat race that close, doesn't want to win!"

Joe Toland went on to say, "He just turned around. And we packed our bags and went home. You did not say to Mr. Kelly, 'Ya, but…' You did not say anything. He was a hard guy, and we knew it and even understood it."

This toughness pierced the Vesper boathouse at 10 East River Drive and was still an influence when our Tokyo eight was being assembled four years after John B. Kelly Sr. had died. His legacy was Jack—'Young Kell'—who took over as the Vesper benefactor and leader in the 1960's.

3

John B. Kelly Jr.

Jack Kelly was born in 1927. The expression that someone was born with silver-spoon-in-mouth could be rewritten for Jack—born with a silver oar in his hands which he strived to make gold.

He lived in the shade of his father, yet in a life that Kelly Senior was anxious first to share and then relinquish. I believe all fathers would like their sons to follow in their footsteps, but few are able to get the young ones to take up a hoped-for inherited interest.

Such was not the Kelly case. The father made it possible for Jack to have the best rowing equipment, the best club, and the best coaching that the sport could nurture. And the son responded.

Having just missed serving in World War II on account of his youth Jack at 19 was ready to compete against the best.

He recalled, "By 1946 rowing in America started to return to normal and I won Vesper's first national sculling championship in many years. I finished second to Jean Sephariades of France in the Diamond Sculls (at England's Henley Regatta). In 1947 I fulfilled my father's dream and won the Diamonds.

"The following year in the Olympic trials, I qualified for the singles. Joe Toland qualified in the pair with cox, but neither of us met with much success.

"My best year was probably 1949, when I won the Diamonds and the European championship. After the Melbourne Olympic of 1956 I retired from rowing the single and rowed entirely in crews. By 1958 we had developed a good eight-oared boat which we sent to Poznan, Poland, for the European Championships where we placed second to Italy. Bill Knecht rowed in the seven seat behind me at stroke, and Allen Rosenberg was our coxswain.

"At this regatta the new rowing club from Ratzeburg in Germany entered their first international eight, and they placed fifth."

Kelly cited Ratzeburg, the club whose considerable successes in the next decade enormously changed training methods, equipment design, and attitudes in our conservative sport.

Like father like son, Jack was devilishly good looking if not quite up to the standard of this his sister Grace. The jaw was a little large.

He had quickly adopted his father's suave style, but never wore it naturally. Jack seemed often to be on a stage like his actress sister, his lines more rehearsed than spontaneous. He had the habit of looking past the person to whom he was talking, as if to measure his effect on a wider audience. Or to insure that he wasn't missing someone more important over there.

Emory Clark, the scribe of our Vesper crew, wrote of Jack, "He was a fine man and a jerk at the same time."

The Kelly clan was sometimes compared to The Kennedy Family due to parallels. Both shared in this common generation the wealthy, self-made patriarchal leader of Irish Catholic background, users of the Democratic Party and ward politics, Joe Kennedy and Jack Senior. The genes brought forth handsome offspring and then alluring mates plus tragic conclusions.

Not everything that Kelly father and son did together was tactful or great. There is an ugly aside to their trip to the Henley regatta in 1946, newspaper photographs of the two standing on the dock holding huge American beefsteaks aloft for all to see. This show of American wealth and strength in battered Britain, so soon after the end of World War II in 1945, was resented by the populous still emerging from five years of strict food rationing—poor diets.

The news clips with pictures were shown to me by English friends at Henley 20 years after the Kelly duo had returned to their regatta, the same regatta to which the father had been denied back in 1920. Jack Jr. won his race in 1947, and the enmity rather than the hearts of the locals.

Joe Toland, the street kid who came into the "new" Vesper Boat Club at the same time as young Jack Kelly, had this insight, "Kell being a winning sculler, the club seemed to revolve around this privileged son."

But it was important at all regattas to win the overall club point championship, which meant that oarsmen had to sometimes row three or four different races in different boats. It could be hot down there in the gulch of the Schuylkill on an oppressive Philadelphia summer afternoon.

"In the years we were trying to build a powerhouse club," said Toland, "Kelly never rowed in any of the tough races. He rowed the single, quad, and the double where nobody was going to beat him. With sculling, he was going to win the national championship and nobody was going to beat him.

"But we wanted to build the other sweep rowing events, especially the eight-oared event. And we needed him. Even as the club's in-your-face agitator, I alone could not convince him to join in rowing the eight, the four-with, or other sweep boats. Kell would always say 'I have a cold.' Or, believe it or not, 'My mother won't let me.'

"So I settled that by telling the coach at the time, Jim Manning, to get Kell's old man in here tomorrow night for practice, and we are going settle this and see who's running this club. Manning was concerned and asked me not to start any trouble, because he needed this coaching job.

"When Mr. Kelly Senior arrived, I was heated up and said to him 'Let's make this short and sweet. Kell doesn't row competitive races. The races he is in, he could swim and win.'

I suggested that if this club is to build, Jack needs to be in tough races.

"'And if they are too tough for him, then they are too tough for me. So what are we going to do?'

"Mr. Kelly looked at his son and said, 'Kid, you are rowing in the eight.' And we went out and won the National Championships."

Toland went on. "Young Kell was an excellent sculler. But his father was hard on him. As an aside to me alone, Mr. Kelly said, 'In every big race he catches a cold.' And for a father to say that about his son to a third party was not loyal. Mr. Kelly was hard on him. He sided with me in many things about young Jack and it was difficult for him to see his son falter where the elder Kelly would have bulled his way to victory.

"Young Jack was the kind of a guy you couldn't dislike. He wasn't a bad guy. He had no meanness. But he did not have the Marine Corps 'follow me' type of leadership either. His father was that kind of a leader and could really kick some ass. But Kell wasn't that guy.

"As a recruiter, a social director, a nice guy, he was super. He really was. Kell needed the pushing that the rest of the Vesper organization gave him."

One vital trait Jack did inherit from his father was the ability to negotiate and to be respected on many levels. He was a hero to his employees and would often visit jobs en route to the boathouse for a morning row. The bricklayers knew that he could do their jobs, as his father had started him in the trenches.

He was fair and respected in the varied ethnic and social arenas of Philadelphia, holding no prejudices. This personality helped him in business, in sports and in politics, all of them entwined. At different times he was president of the Amateur Athletic Union of America and its occasional antagonist, the U.S. Olympic Committee.

Of course he served on the board of directors of the National Association of Amateur Oarsmen, the organization that authorized the first Vesper trip to the Olympics back in 1900. He left the lovable Doc Riggall with the precious title as president of Vesper while he acted as secretary/treasurer, often balancing the books with a personal deposit.

Vesper in these years was building a strong attitude that would carry the club into the 1964 challenge. Jack Kelly Jr. was the carrier of that load of bricks upward, building the structure that would soon astonish the world of sport.

4

It Began With Bill Knecht

When John B. Kelly Senior brought Philadelphia's LaSalle High School into Vesper to build his stable of rowing racers, Bill Knecht was introduced to his new life sport. At first a commuting student from New Jersey, Bill later became the oldest and most experienced oarsman in our 1964 Olympic eight.

Rowing along with Joe Toland and in the shadow of Jack Kelly, Bill Knecht became a quiet but fierce racer. According to Bill's wife Joan, he looked up to the senior Kelly as the father he never had.

He both envied and admired young Jack and supported him in his quest to become the world's leading sculler, often sparring with him on the river in the single, pushing him but never discouraging him by beating him.

They were close friends for life, each being the godfather of the other's son. Bill Knecht was satisfied being in the shadow of Jack, and this extended family was a comfort to him. Kelly was his model, and Bill was always willing to be a step behind him. Yet those knowledgeable in rowing circles are sure that Knecht was the better sculler.

Joe Toland had this to say about his friend Bill Knecht. "He was a very good basketball player and also played football for LaSalle. As a rower he won the high school championship in his junior and senior years and won the Canadian schoolboy championship in his junior year as well. He was a good oarsman, better than Kelly. But there was a problem.

"Coach Jim Manning was on the Kelly payroll and he felt pressure to have young Jack be the star of the boathouse. That is how Manning made his living, and it would never do to coach another to beat Jack."

So Toland took over the responsibility of coaching Bill Knecht and they did it quietly, sneaking out of the boathouse for workouts. Toland said, "Bill and I used to go out on the river when it was still dark in the morning. Sometimes we would have to cut the chain on the coaching motorboat in order to use it.

"Later in the day Jim Manning might ask me, 'How is that Knecht going?' And I would tell him that he is the fastest guy that ever rowed on this river. Someone said it was too bad you couldn't put a wall down in the middle of the river and have Knecht on one side and Kelly on the other, because when he sits on that starting line where he can watch Kelly he is not going to go that fast. He would subconsciously choke in a big race with Kelly and not follow the determined race plan. But Bill was a hell of an oarsman. He could row a boat.

"Knecht adored Kelly. Jack's life style and being a playboy, he just so admired that. He didn't have the charm with women that Kelly had. Bill had a lot more talent than Kelly in business and probably over all in rowing. He was president of the Sheet Metal Workers Union, the contractors' association. Bill was a good guy at everything he did. A team player.

"His weakness? He wasn't totally his own man. I saw him do so many good things for people, it was unreal. He just couldn't get past Kelly. If Jack jumped off a bridge, Bill would be right behind him."

For the 1960 Rome Olympics, Bill rowed in the double with Kelly. Illness eliminated their chances at success, and unfortunately it was Bill who became sick. That was Jack's final elite race, but Bill was determined to continue. He loved rowing and racing and figured he had another four years in him.

Fellow Vesper oarsman Emory Clark, in summing up his impressions of Knecht, has written, "Knecht didn't look much of a physical specimen. But as a big barrel of a man he certainly was a heavyweight. Looks can be deceiving as he, among other things, was the best pure oarsman in the club. He had been in various Vesper eights in the 1950s, rowing either port or starboard sides, and had for many years been the national quarter-mile sprint sculling champion. That was an event Jack Kelly would not enter. Long on experience, he knew what it took to get himself in shape and how to effectively move a boat with his oar.

"I used to think at times he was goofing off—not rowing as hard as I was during workouts. But I kept my own counsel, figuring he knew what he was doing. Later I looked to Knecht for leadership but he never really assumed that role. I think he had seen so much club rowing in 16 years that the disorganization and squabbling did not affect him one way or another. I was not sure who he thought he would row with that year, since Kelly had retired. But 1964 was clearly to be his last hurrah."

I agree that Bill Knecht was a great rower and when he sat behind me in the seven seat, I had total confidence in him. He was a stroke counter and at any time during a race he knew exactly where the boat was because he had been counting strokes from the start. Depending on the wind and the competition, we knew that a race of 2000 meters would take 230 strokes. So Bill always knew when it was time to sprint. Bill was a picture of concentration on the water and he kept to himself, delivering the very best. He became my trip roommate and the person I was the closest to on the crew.

His intensity was incredible, and it was not until the last months of his life that he was diagnosed as a manic depressive. This condition is hereditary and both his brother and his son have suffered much worse consequences from it, including hospitalization. According to his wife Joan, he self-medicated himself with total immersion in either rowing, his contracting business, wine and women, or various combinations of these.

Bill was balancing twice-a-day rowing workouts, a multimillion dollar sheet metal contracting business, the family, and the commuting between the three. I only knew of the rowing and his work.

He placed incredible strain on Joan because he prioritized rowing over family life, and the raising of six children alone was a huge task. Yet she supported him in his habit. As angry as she would get over his rowing, she would be on the shore screaming for him to win at every regatta. And then host the whole team at the Knecht home for a victory party.

Bill's total involvement, and ability to reach success, apparently kept his mental disorder under control. Joan was relieved when Bill retired from active racing because she believed he would have the time to help with the family.

Imagine her disappointment when he announced to her, on the airplane returning from Tokyo, that it was his time to "pay back" to rowing what he took from it. He launched himself into a time-consuming volunteer career as president of the National Association of Amateur Oarsmen; as the American delegate to F.I.S.A., the world rowing governing body; as one of the founders of the National Rowing Foundation, and as the creator of the new rowing course on the Cooper River in Camden, New Jersey. Additionally he accepted more responsibility for his business and various trade organizations.

Bill Knecht had met Joan while on a summer Vesper rowing trip to Michigan's Wyandotte Boat Club. It seems that Joan had a cousin, her Uncle Will's son, who also went to LaSalle in Philadelphia and so the traveling team imposed on the hospitality of Joan's family for a picnic.

Young Bill Knecht was a senior at LaSalle and had plans to continue his Catholic education at Villanova University when he met seventeen-year old Joan at this picnic. He asked her if he could write her and the correspondence romance began.

Three years later elaborate wedding plans were upset by the start of the Korean War. Bill and Joan scrapped the formal wedding for a quick one the night before he reported for military service as a conscript recruit. Joan was 20 years old. They called upon Pat Costello, the Detroit Boat Club's sculler, to be best man and then Bill was off to serve his country. The first of their six children was born the following year. Jack Kelly only had five kids, meaning that Knecht won this race with Kelly. But Joan adds that she cheated by having a set of twins.

It was impossible to dislike Bill Knecht. He was simply a very good man as we measured him. He was the senior man and we all respected him greatly. Although he did not take a leadership role in our eight everyone buttoned up and listened when he spoke. He was the prefect seven man. As his stroke of the Vesper eight, I was forever grateful to have had Bill Knecht backing me up.

5

Rosenberg, Second On Board

Allen Rosenberg was introduced to Vesper Boat Club during Christmas of 1953. He was working as a holiday spare in the Philadelphia post office when another part time worker, an oarsman from Cornell University, asked if he had ever been a coxswain for the Big Red. Al said no, he'd never been to Cornell and was told he looked just like a guy there who steered boats. Might Al want to try coxing?

"I told him it would be fun to think about," said Rosenberg. "At the time I weighed 95 pounds and was 22 years old. He said why didn't I come down to the Vesper boathouse this weekend as they were going to have a big Christmas party and I could meet the guys.

"So I went down to the club, came up the old rickety steps, pushed open the door and walked into the bar room. I recollect there were about six guys, big big guys. They had their backs to the door. They turned around and said, 'Here he is, here he is.' They were waiting for me.

"So in January and February of 1954 I went to Vesper every day waiting for the opportunity to take a boat out. It was cold, very cold. I didn't get a boat to steer at Vesper, and the wonderful University of Pennsylvania coach, Joe Burk, would see me standing on the dock every day. Then he let me take out one of his boats.

"The very first boat I steered was the Penn third varsity, which on that day only had six men in it. They were the leftover men in the boathouse. Joe Burk was happy to have me since little coxswains were scarce, especially in the cold of winter. I did not know diddley squat about coxing and I held the rudder ropes, leaning forward, like a fighter, pulling against the rudder so it would stay straight. I came back from the practice and my back hurt, my neck hurt. Then someone suggested I ease up, just sit there and steer. That was my introduction to rowing."

A feisty little Jewish boy in an Irish-Catholic club might have had problems in the 1950's, but any prejudices at 100 pounds were overlooked. That summer of

1954 Allen coxed the Vesper four with coxswain which won a national championship on Lake Quinsigamond in Worcester, Massachusetts.

Joe Toland was in the boat. With that victory came the opportunity to race at the Pan American Games, to be held in Mexico City in March of 1955. The Vesper four took a silver medal behind the crew from Argentina which went on to win the more difficult European championship that year.

Rosenberg must have been a natural. He also coxed the eight to a gold medal victory in those Pan Am Games, with Bill Knecht at stroke and Joe Toland rowing seven. Al attributes his much of his success to his mentors, Toland and the Vesper coach, Jim Manning.

Allen was in his senior year at the Temple University School of Pharmacy and then attended law school at Temple. When I suggested that Allen might be a Temple kind of guy, he responded, "My mother always said go to Temple. So I did.

"It was a brutal schedule for me because I was working during the day, would hop a ride at 5 p.m. to the East River Drive, get in boats to steer until 6:30, jump in my car there and take the shortcut to Broad and Columbia Streets for law school, where I was invariably late for every class. For four years I had that schedule without a break."

Rosenberg had gone to Philadelphia's Central High School, the second oldest public high school in America. He tried out for track but was deemed too small for the varsity squad. He did win his class numerals as a quarter-miler and he also wrestled some as a Temple undergraduate. Although Al was a prime candidate for a coxswain, Temple did not have a rowing program until many years later.

For Allen Rosenberg it was not enough that he be the little guy steering the boat. He became a fastidious student of the sport, soaking up all he could about rowing.

After a decent career as a coxswain he became briefly the rowing coach at St. Joseph's College in Philadelphia, a part time position. Anxious to get a full time paying career, Allen took a patent lawyers position with a pharmaceutical company, Miles Laboratory in Elkhart, Indiana where crew was all but unknown. He remained in relative rowing obscurity until 1963 when he was called by Jack Kelly to return to Vesper to become the head coach.

Emory Clark remembers the Al Rosenberg of 1963 as, "A man with all sorts of complexes, Jewish, a little man, and later when he was married, a man/woman complex. But Al was a rowing genius. At the same time he was abrasive, demanding and arrogant. So he always had the rest of the rowing world mad at him, because of jealousy over his talent and success or because he had managed an alienation by some outrageous demand."

Clark supposes that Kelly had taken on Rosenberg, for a fulltime well-paid job, to see if Allen could harness the Amlong brothers to do something useful for Vesper. You, dear reader, will soon meet up with Joe and Tom Amlong.

From my standpoint, Rosenberg was a totally different coach than any I had known. That included the great Stork Sanford of Cornell, the ultimate mentor of the long layback style favored by the long bladed sweep oarsmen of the 1920's and on into the early 1960's. Sanford's foundation was the classic swing style he head learned as an undergraduate at the University of Washington, the famous Conibear stroke named after Hiram Conibear, an early Husky coach in Seattle.

Rosenberg's stroke kept only the length but he even modified that.

For all previous coaches I had given my total respect and absolute belief in their methods, never questioning their wisdom or what they told me. Al would not only tell you what to do, but why you were doing it. If he wanted to change something in your style, he could verbalize it in three or more totally different ways, one of which was sure to catch.

Al and I spent time over a kitchen sink with a spoon, me being shown why we attacked the water as we did with the oar. He treated oarsmen as his equals and taught in a mature and adult manner. I learned more from Al than I had ever learned before. Perhaps that was my fault because as a schoolboy and college oarsman I had been content to do what I was told. Only with athletic maturity came curiosity.

For example, I had always thought that oarsmen were supposed to rip the oar through the water, pulling as hard as possible to get to the end of the stroke cycle. After some discussion with Al I finally realized that you were to plant or anchor the oar in the water and move the boat past that anchor.

With these new thoughts I could understand the new equipment that we were asked to use. The hull design of our shell from Italy was different than the home grown American boats that we had been rowing for years.

Back to the kitchen sink with a plate in the water to show how the vee hull of our boat rose up at a higher stroke, thus causing less wetted surface of resistance than the conventional U-shaped flat-bottom hulls. I found I had become a part of the thinking process and not just a pawn in a boat.

Allen read everything possible about all sports and borrowed training methods and ideas from others like the famous Indiana swimming coach, Doc Counsilman, or track innovator Fred Wilt. Allen knew why a karate expert could break bricks with his hands, and he applied this application of strength to our putting the oar in the water.

As a pharmacist he had ideas about what non-prescription vitamins and natural food supplements should be taken to enhance performance. Perhaps I should have questioned the pills he gave us, but I had total trust in his judgment. The physical mechanics and functions of the body were putty in his hands. He knew when and how to get the best performances from his players and was careful not to overtrain which would create staleness. Time and again he brought us to our peak of conditioning.

With younger oarsmen he might have had a bit more trouble with psyche, but he was able to handle mature and motivated athletes with ease.

Allen came in at the right time and was the perfect coach of the Vesper quest for Olympic excellence.

6

Robert Zimonyi, Coxswain Supreme

The 1964 Olympic eight from Vesper was regarded as a diverse group of mostly determined young men. But young was not truly so. In addition to 34-year-old Bill Knecht, the coxswain steering the American shell down the Toda Rowing Course in Tokyo was 46 years old, a truly 'old man' in the collegiate circles that had dominated the sport in America. Unlikely, unheard of!

Coxswain Robert Zimonyi, who defected from Hungary at the time of the 1956 Olympic Games in Australia, had the most colorful background of the entire American team. Born in Sarvar, Hungary, on April 18th, 1918, Robby was the oldest active athlete on the 1964 American Olympic team. He began with the sport in high school in 1934, at the age 14 when a friend dragged him to the boathouse. The coach there saw a perfect potential coxswain. Robby never grew and always tipped the scales at the minimum 50 kilos (110 pounds), sparing his oarsmen the burden of pulling extra weight down the course.

In the 1948 London Olympic games Robby coxed the Hungarian pair with coxswain to a third-place bronze medal. In the 1952 Helsinki Olympics he steered the Hungarian eight, narrowly missing the medals with a fourth-place finish. The Melbourne Olympics in 1956 found the Hungarian team's concentration shattered by the Soviet invasion and subsequent riots at home during the competitions. Numerous Hungarian athletes and coaches preferred to take the opportunity to start a new life of freedom rather than return to Hungary with its questionable Communist future.

Jack Kelly, our Vesper sculler who had just won the bronze medal in Melbourne, had the time and the heart to help numerous Hungarian athletes find refuge in America. He worked with them and obtained permission for several to come to the United States. Among these men was Robert Zimonyi, coxswain supreme.

The Kelly group of defectors arrived in Philadelphia on Christmas Day, 1956, and Jack began to find jobs, helping them begin a new life. According to Allen Rosenberg, "A group of these men made their first American home the Vesper Boat Club. For two months they occupied the bar room and the third floor of the club, dividing the space between their cots by hanging flannel sheets on clothes lines. As Kell found them jobs and an income they moved out into the community."

Isabel Gressner, Robert's wonderful lady friend for over 40 years, recalled that his first job in the United States was with Kelly's brick company. It was hardly a suitable position for a 110-pound former accountant, and Kelly helped him get a job with friends as a clerk for the General Public Warehouse. When that company was acquired and lost its Philadelphia identity, a friend of Robert introduced him to the Sandmeyer family and he became an accountant for the Sandmeyer Steel Company, a position he held from 1963 until he retired in 1983. Isabel said, "The Sandmeyers were his second family and they were wonderful to him. A beautiful family."

Robby Zimonyi did not immediately take to the water for Vesper, primarily because he could not speak English. It took him four years to gain the language confidence necessary to be an asset to the club.

Dr. Sean Shea remembers rowing in the Vesper junior four-with-coxswain in the Schuylkill Navy Regatta of June 18th, 1960, Zimonyi's first experience winning an American boat race. Said Sean, "We were just four high school kids and we were pissed that coach Jim Manning gave us an old-man coxswain who couldn't even speak English, and barely tried to talk to us." They finished first in spite of this handicap, never supposing that this "old man" would someday shine as the best coxswain in the world.

Rosenberg says that Zimonyi would often resort to calling commands in Hungarian when he got deep into an event during his early Vesper races. But, adds Allen, "Zimonyi was the best. He was unflappable, a truly marvelous coxswain. And his steering was always perfect. After workouts we would have conferences in my boathouse apartment and Robby would come in for a smoke and say, 'I tink I vil have a coffee now.' Then he would give me great insight into the intricacies of the delicate shell and the men moving it. He had a keen sense of knowing what was wrong and who was causing the problems, yet he had a difficult time expressing it on the water."

As the stroke of our Vesper eight, I sat the closest to Robby and we had an excellent face to face working relationship, I communicating in grunts and facial expressions. He was also a great companion out of the shell and we would always sit together when traveling on airplanes where I would eat most of his meals. His stomach was smaller and he had to pretend that he was working to keep his weight down. In exchange for extra food, I would overlook his smoking habit.

The only difficulty that I ever had with Robby was the time I laughed as he told me that George Washington was a Hungarian. He got very annoyed with me and after that I did not bring it up, unless I wanted to get his goat. To this day, I have no idea what he was talking about. I took the trouble, almost 40 years after the statement, to look up Washington's genealogy and found that his roots have been traced back to 1260 in England where Sulgrave Manor is regarded as the home of George Washington's ancestors. I found that the name Washington was derived from deWessington, which does not sound too Hungarian to me. George Washington or no George Washington, Robert Zimonyi became a citizen of the United States in 1962.

In junior and college boats the coxswain is more of an auxiliary coach and a cheerleader but as oarsmen gain experience and racing maturity this role is not as critical. Emory Clark summed it up saying, "Most college oarsmen who rowed in eights took the steering for granted until their coxswain went off course or hit a buoy. It was a great comfort for us to have someone you could count on not to lose you 1/100th of a second with his steering, someone whom the glamour, excitement and psyche of a major regatta meant no increase in the pulse.

"If Robby was not the spiritual leader of the crew, if he did not embody the ego of the boat, if he did not possess the intangible quality of spirit which lifts a crew to heights beyond its capability, it did not matter. We didn't need it. We were hungry elders and we had it within ourselves. We needed Robby's experience, his calm, his competence, his ability to steer. At 46 he had seen it all before."

These qualities were what made this old man a key player in the success of the 1964 crew.

7

The Eccentric Amlong Brothers

Rusty Callow, the grand rowing coach at Penn and Navy and a splendid rowing philosopher, once said, "I have never met an oarsman that I didn't like." But Callow never met the Amlong brothers, Joe and Tom.

Before any of my negative sentences, and there will be a few, I need admit that they were two fierce competitors, as strong of body as they were bull-headed of mind, dedicated to whatever cause they happened to stumble upon. Joe and Tom, oarsmen of note, were hardly nice guys and they made little attempt to be nice guys. They basked in their idiosyncrasies and caused discomfort to people with whom they came in contact.

Much could be written about their exploits. While not close friends of mine, I was always happy that they were rowing in our boat with me and not in another against me.

They had arrived at the Vesper in 1961, the next in order of the characters joining that boat club's scene in the quest for 1964 excellence. While others in my chronicle are presented as individuals—each a unique building block—the Amlongs must be treated as one. They were a pair and to be effective they had to be together, like bookends. To separate them here would be a duplicity.

Tom is the older, by fifteen months. They came from an Army family raised on military bases with Joe born in Haines, Alaska, and Tom in Fort Knox, Kentucky. Their introduction to rowing came by coincidence in 1951 at Liege, Belgium, where their father, a colonel in the Army, was in charge of an on-going World War II graves registration unit. He was the post commander.

In lieu of sending their boys away to a private school somewhere, the Amlong parents chose to educate their five sons at home. They bought five desks and enrolled the boys in a University of Nebraska extension program designed for rural, remote farm children. Given the circumstances home schooling may have been the right choice. But it did not teach social mixing nor did it present any athletic opportunities.

From the windows of their eighth-floor lodging—or fourth floor depending on the brother telling the story—they could see Belgians rowing up and down upon the canal below them.

The brothers sensed that rowing would be neat, so Dad the Colonel loaded them into their Pontiac station wagon one Sunday to visit—and to join—the Union Audi Boat Club one mile up the canal. The puzzled Belgians put four of the Amlong brothers, ages 13, 15, 17 and 18, into a training barge, wood, heavy, large, wide and with staggered seats. Because the eldest brother was 18, they had to row in the 18-and-over class, but they gained some exposure and had their pictures in the newspaper. The publicity hooked Joe and Tom.

Colonel Amlong believed that young men should honor their military obligations and soon it was 1950, with the Korean War at hand. Two brothers Jerry and Mike, were sent off to join the Air Force leaving Joe and Tom alone to row in a pair.

Tom now claims, "One of the reasons we started to row was because there were some good looking girls playing on the rowing club basketball team. And Belgian girls rowed too."

In September, 1951, Colonel Amlong was transferred to Bremerhaven, Germany, and the boys were enrolled in the American School for Dependents. Tom said, "We joined the Bremerhaven Rudersport Club and actually learned to speak German. The coach wanted me to go into the eight. But because he thought Joe was rowing without using his back properly, he excluded him from the boat. We then convinced Mom that she should buy us a double so we could row together."

A plywood double was purchased and at first they did well in age-group racing. But when they hit open competition they were badly beaten.

Joe said, "One time we ran straight into two German kids in a kayak, and destroyed the bow third of our new double scull. Tom and I jumped into the water and started to beat up on these kids. They were bigger than us. But we were mad about wrecking our shell."

As their rowing careers progressed other boats got out of the way and so the Amlong brothers avoided collisions. In time they moderated their aggressiveness toward others but were known to fight one another while on the water in the double. They could be heard.

Soon after the boat repair had been completed the Amlong family was transferred back to the United States, settling in Alexandria, Virginia. Tom and Joe quickly found their way to the nearby Old Dominion Boat Club where they muscled into the club's junior eight. This was the summer of 1954. At a regatta in Philadelphia that boat advanced through the Intermediate class before they were destroyed by a Vesper senior eight with Jack Kelly in it.

On August 18, 1954, the brothers took themselves out of rowing by enlisting in the Army, joining the 82nd Airborne Division. Jump school among the lean mean paratroopers did nothing to hone their sociable skills.

The U.S. Department of Defense had adopted a policy of encouraging aspiring American athletes in the military to apply for special assignment to enable them to train as Olympic candidates. Tom and Joe applied, were accepted, and in 1955 found themselves stationed in Washington, D.C., where they could train on the Potomac River for the 1956 Olympic trials.

The Amlongs had for idols the 1952 U.S. Olympic champion pair of Chuck Logg and Henry (Hank) Price, and Joe and Tom figured their best chance to go somewhere in international rowing was in a similar pair-without-coxswain.

In their beginnings they had some success and then discovered that the best athletes appeared in the serious Olympic years. Their inflated egos burst when they were humiliated by Jim Fifer and Duvall Hecht in the U.S. Olympic trials. When Fifer and Hecht became Olympic champions in Melbourne in the fall of 1956, the Amlong pair had become college students.

After being rejected by the Naval Academy, Joe accepted an appointment to the United States Military Academy at West Point. He had hoped to row for Navy and coach Rusty Callow, but was rejected by the plebe recruiter because he believed at only 6 foot tall he was "too short to row for Navy."

Tom first enrolled at the University of Maryland and a year later transferred to Virginia. While none of these institutions had rowing programs the brothers committed themselves to year-around work-out programs. When another opportunity came around, they would be ready.

In Allen Rosenberg's opinion, Joe Amlong "came the closest that we had in the 1964 Vesper boat to being a natural athlete." That wasn't apparent to coaches at the Military Academy. Perhaps because of the home schooling abroad Joe lacked the skills in baseball, basketball or football that might have enabled him to qualify for a significant team at Army.

He said of the Military Academy experience, "When I went out for football, I had been training for the 1956 Olympics and I was really in good shape. I went out to the field and old Earl Blaik (Army's famous football coach) and the team were laughing at me because I didn't have on my hip pads. I didn't know that much about football. They made me run back to the gym and get some hip pads on. When I returned they were all laughing at me because I didn't have the belt on. So they made me run the half mile back to the gym again to get a belt. When I got back to the field they must have said, 'Let's have some fun with this clown.'

"So they made a round robin where they all stand around and you stand in the middle and a guy comes out and hits you. Then as soon as he hits you, another guy comes out and hits you. In those days in football you were considered a candy ass if you wore a plastic face mask.

"You were allowed to use a head-up block, which is now illegal. It's where you can have your chin all the way tucked under and hit a man with your forehead.

"They put me in this round robin but I had done some boxing and knew how to use my elbow. I knocked three guys out cold. That qualified me as a starting guard on the freshman team that season. The guys didn't like me very well. So I found myself getting clipped. Knee injury and out for the season."

Joe soldiered along. "I would not quit and (next season) played on the varsity meatball squad. I played for the trips, the chance to get away from the rigors of West Point. We got to go to town. I did not suit up for the varsity games but played a lot of B squad games. I didn't have the skills or football knowledge that the others had. We played a lot of little colleges and we used to cream them. The amazing thing was that I was a guard and I made more touchdowns than anyone else on the team by picking up fumbles. And the reason was we played so rough that it would shake up the other team's center to the point of no return and you could take the football right out of his hands.

"It was almost impossible to break in the varsity as a walk-on like me because the assistant coaches had done their recruiting in Pennsylvania and like that, and they wanted to keep their recruited kids in the those slots. The only way to move up was to injure the one in front of you."

Joe also boxed at West Point in the cadet corps intramural competition. Even with the fat 16-ounce gloves, Joe had five straight knockouts in the unlimited heavyweight division although weighing 183. He was eliminated in the tournament, he said, by a 230-pound shot-putter. Among his peers, he had made a name for himself.

It all sounds a little crazy to me. I am grateful for such tough Army training and grateful that Joe Amlong was on my side.

In 1961 Joe graduated from West Point and, having 60 days of leave time, he asked Tom if he wanted to row. Tom replied, "Hell yes. But I'm not going to row for Old Dominion. I'm going to Philadelphia and join up with Jack Kelly."

"Vesper was the only club putting out fast boats," Tom remembered. "The rest of them only had good bars. Vesper didn't have much of a bar but they were more serious. They had coach Jim Manning and he was smart. Joe and I got to be good buddies with Al Nino, the club trainer, because we were muscle heads. I think Al was a bodyguard for Kelly, but he took us under his wing and we worked out at the Philadelphia Athletic Club when not on the water."

While the brothers Amlong seem to have volunteered, as they tell their story, I know by separate lore that they were welcomed as though expected and even recruited. I also think that they confirmed the conviction of both Kelly and Rosenberg that Vesper could build an Olympic eight to beat the best college crews. Besides Bill Knecht, whom we always took for granted, the rest of us have the Amlongs to thank that they tipped the balance, gave the Vesper venture some substance.

In 1961 the Amlong brothers lived in the attic of the Vesper Boat Club and worked for Kelly. "Tom and I were lugging cinder blocks and moving scaffolding for building the new Philadelphia stadium," said Joe. "We had to take a shower before rowing because our crotch and armpits were full of sand. We had to keep our heads up because the regular bricklayers knew we were some of Kelly's college boys and they were always throwing bricks off the scaffolding to scare us. As an officer in the Air Force I was not supposed to be moonlighting but the $3.75 an hour on top of officers' pay, made the hard work worthwhile."

The disputatious brothers were also gaining notoriety. They traveled to races in an old car with the boat racked above it and they cooked meals in a filthy pot over the heat of the engine block. Then they used the military athletes assistance program to be assigned together for awhile. "Tom was stationed in Yuma, Arizona and I was in Myrtle Beach, South Carolina," said Joe. "I got the Air Force to move me to Yuma so we could train together. We rented a little shack near the Colorado River where we rowed the pair. Then the Army released Tom from what he was doing and we both got transferred back to Philadelphia where we could get some coaching." The brothers Amlong might arrange to row together but they were not building much of a military career path.

Perhaps a low point in the Amlong entry into the gentlemanly sport of rowing came at the 1963 Henley Royal Regatta. They conned their way to Europe aboard a MATS (Military Air Transport System) flight and borrowed a shell. "The boat was like a waterlogged mattress," Tom said. "It was so old and beat up. After we complained the news media found out and Joe and I were not very astute in handling the press. The newspapers came out and said that those spoiled American brats did not like the equipment so graciously lent them.

"At the same time Mohammed Ali was about to have a fight with some English boxer and we were compared to him with his really bad press. We were finally given a better boat, but in the final race at Henley the referee must have gotten the names of the crews mixed up and he kept repeating for Vesper to get in the correct lane, which we in fact were. This so unnerved us that we moved over and hit the log boom that delineates the course. This of course allowed the favored English crew to get by us and win the race.

"After the race we lodged a protest and all this got in the press and it was a big story because in my opinion the regatta was boring anyway and we were the only story available. When we returned to the United States we found that the National Association of Amateur Oarsmen had picked up on the story and they showed their displeasure with our attitude by banning us from rowing for awhile."

Perhaps that explains why our crew, when we finally got to Tokyo for the Olympics, was instructed that only Rosenberg or myself were to talk to the press as spokesmen for the group.

Joe got married, on August 12, 1963, and to this day Tom resents Gail because she took his brother away. Tom went ballistic, according to Joe. "He called the boatbuilder, Stan Pocock in Seattle, and ordered a single so he could row alone without me."

To their credit the brothers Amlong were students of what others were doing, what equipment they were using and how they rigged their boats. Americans as a whole did not concern themselves with boat rigging, and left that to the builder, while the Europeans were gaining sophistication and speed by customizing the rigging to accommodate each oarsman. Charlie Butt, the astute coach of the Potomac Boat Club, has said, "The Amlongs were pioneers in collecting and applying this kind of data to their shells."

Along the way they drove people crazy with their personal theories about how everyone should rig their boats and how wrong most others were.

Emory Clark had a summation of the brothers Amlong. "They were short—maybe a little over six feet—and each a solid 200 pounds, enormously powerful with slabs of muscle everywhere including their brains. They were antagonistic and contemptuous of everyone, including each other, legendary for their lack of tact."

We all had our favorite Amlong stories. "They were crude to the extreme in sexual matters, Tom in a general graphic sort of way, Joe in a more specific manner," said Clark. "One was never in doubt of either's sexual prowess. Every day, after they got in the boat somewhere during the workout, we learned of Joe's sexual activity from the night before, like 'Took my old lady on the kitchen table last night." Or, 'We did it on the edge of the kitchen sink with the water running.'

"While my sex life was not entirely non existent it was nowhere near as spectacular as Joe's. Nor did I share it on a regular basis with Boat House Row. It is perhaps indelicate and distasteful to recall these things now but they were such a part of the climate of our crew and its practices that any story would be incomplete without them."

As the stroke of the crew aft, with Joe and Tom sitting up toward the bow, I could not hear and thus was saved such tidings as Emory reported. Maybe I was old fashioned but the contention that sexual activity would sap your strength remained on my mind and I attempted to tell Joe that perhaps he should save something to help make the boat go faster. I recall after a particularly good practice Joe asked everyone in the locker room what they thought of that evening's row. Upon receiving unanimous acclaim that the boat was flying, Joe proceeded to give a graphic description of his luncheon mating with his wife, proving to himself once and for all that I was wrong about abstinence during training.

Emory Clark had another insight. "Tom and Joe were real animals, altogether obnoxious characters who had the facility of having everyone mad at them three-quarters of the time. But whom I nonetheless found hard not to like sometimes. Tom in particular made an effort to be nasty. It was his theory that you would row harder if you were nervous, angry, upset.

"The most important attribute of the Amlongs was that they were very fast in their pair. Granted they could never seem to beat anyone consistently over a 2,000-meter race but that was because they consistently psyched themselves out.

"Or because Tom, angry for some reason at Joe, would stop rowing, turn around and hit Joe, who of course would falter in his stroke. By the time they got straightened out, some lesser pair would have an insurmountable lead.

"They were determined to row their pair where they felt they had the best chance of making the Olympic team. For a long time they refused to row in the Vesper eight because—to use their term—it was full of pussies, a direct reference to female anatomy which loomed large in their thinking and speech."

While the Amlongs made rowing for Vesper interesting, sometimes amusing, they did not make it fun. The laughter one might derive from their antics could not overcome the anguish from their being inconsiderate, rude, and obnoxious. I found it was best to distance myself from them. The occasions when I found myself in a confrontation, I simply walked away. When they questioned my ability as the stroke, I told them as long as I was sitting in the eight seat I would set the pace and if they did not like it, 'Take it up with the coach and get me removed.'"

My bluff worked and I had few problems with them. No one socialized with the Amlongs. I respected what they did when we were "all together" in the boat but can say little good about our life on the shore together.

Dr. Sean Shea observed the following about these beasts of the Vesper boathouse: "They were good oarsmen. However they had a negative effect on a lot of others and I never remember them trying to help anybody, to make them better. They always denigrated everyone, calling them pussies or something demeaning. They were totally self-centered, never a positive factor. But you can't get away from the fact that they were very good oarsmen."

Yes, but they were just two of the twelve Vesper characters that constituted the miracle in Tokyo. So let's drift away from them and get on with the rest of the boat.

8

A Rose Arrives from Germany

When the West German Olympic eight won at the Rome Olympic Games in 1960, it was the first time since 1912 that any crew other than one from an American university had captured rowing's outstanding event. American heads spun after the youngsters from an obscure club in Ratzeburg of the German Federal Republic snared the gold medals. The U.S. entry of Midshipmen from the Naval Academy was a disappointing fifth, the worst showing ever of an American eight-oared Olympic crew.

What did the Americans do following such a drubbing? Not much in either 1961 or 1962. By 1963 those in charge realized something was wrong about the way our crews were rowing the short sprint distance of 2,000 meters, the international standard of about a mile and a quarter. So the victorious Ratzeburg crew was invited to visit and race some of the eastern college eights.

I missed the excitement, being an Ensign in Vietnam running the Saigon Officers Club. I understand that cameras rolled and clicked as the Germans won themselves a lot of ink on the sports pages. Their rowing stroke was meticulously analyzed but the copying Americans seemed to go even slower than before. Our coaches attempted vainly to follow the lead of Karl Adam, the renowned German mentor.

Two problems arose. The Americans were changing their rowing style to conform with the fast Europeans but did not use the same measurements in the equipment that properly enabled such style changes. Furthermore, they were still using training routines that had been successful for our traditional longer races of two, three and even four miles. The American coaches did not shift their methods appropriate to the shorter and higher-stroking sprint event.

After taking yards of film of the Ratzeburg crew training on Lake Carnegie, Princeton coach Delos (Dutch) Schoch analyzed the body movements and attempted to reproduce them while staying with the conventional American equipment produced for decades by the Pocock family of Seattle.

Schoch reduced the body swing of the crew to conform with that of the German champions but he did not increase the length of the sliding seat tracks. He attempted to increase the strokes per minute but did not adjust the length of the oar and the position of the button on the oar. So the poor Princeton oarsmen were attempting to row at a higher cadence with a heavy leveraged oar. My explanation may be confusing but the result was not. The copycat crews struggled.

Earlier in 1963 the ninth best oarsman in the Ratzeburg stable of rowers decided to abandon the German club because he could not make the eight, and Vesper's Jack Kelly was quick to have him to come to America. Thus Dietrich Rose arrived in Philadelphia in April, 1963 and with him came a wealth of information about the successful Ratzeburg rowing techniques.

Dietrich was born on August 31, 1936, in Ruedersdorf, a small resort town about 20 miles outside of Berlin where the Olympic Games were being held. He once told me, "I saw Jesse Owens, the American sprinter, win a gold medal from inside my mother's belly. He was running and I was kicking."

The family had a restaurant and boat rental business appropriately called The Rose Garden. Dietrich's first rowing experience was ferrying customers across the river, at age six. World War II in Germany proved difficult and his conscripted soldier father was captured and held in a British prisoner of war camp for six months at the end of the war. The father swam the Elbe River so as to be captured by the British instead of the Soviets.

When asked about his part in the war effort, Dietrich didn't hesitate with his answer. "Of course I was too young to be a member of the Hitler Youth, and would have had to wait a year to join. But I was ready to go. I had the uniform, the credentials, and was looking forward. It was a German effort and I was an influenced nine year old.

"These were difficult times. You don't know what it is to be hungry. We ate berries to fill our stomachs. After the war had ended my father lost his job as an accountant because he had been a member of the Nazi party. He took a job as a stove fitter, building ceramic stoves for apartments."

There was a rowing club six miles away and his first competitive experience was as a coxswain. The year was 1952. But Rose soon was too big for steering and started sweep rowing. Earlier that year his family had separated, his mother and brothers living in the East German sector of Berlin while Dietrich and his father took up residence in the western section where there was a better school for young Rose. The family was not reunited in the west sector until 1954.

Dietrich tells a favorite story about his discovery of the building of the Berlin Wall by the East Germans when he was rowing for Ratzeburg in Potsdam in

1961. He said, "We were racing in the final selection to make the European championship team when we heard tanks rolling during the night on the road outside the barracks where we were housed.

"The next morning there were East German soldiers with machine guns in the starting stake boats, and they told us—incorrectly as it turned out—that we would not be able to return home due to the new regulations and The Wall that had been built over night. We lost the race and for the first time in my life I cried."

While the Americans had been savoring their reputation as the source of world's best eight-oared crews, the West German coach Karl Adam was experimenting with different equipment and training methods. He was a teacher of mathematics in the North German village of Ratzeburg and he had never rowed.

Adam applied common mathematical sense to our sport in building a better boat and developing new oar-blade designs. He also brought to rowing the modern interval training methods utilized by track coaches.

He began with a group of high school boys from this village in Northern Germany and ended up with a dynasty of tall, hugely built Olympic champions. Rose, seeking to row with the best, had moved to Ratzeburg from Hamburg to learn under Adam and he contributed his mechanical engineering expertise to help his new coach design better rigging and oars.

But Dietrich made one mistake. Knowing that he had to be away from the practice area early one spring weekend Rose asked his friend Horst Meyer to fill in. The boat went better and Coach Adam kept Meyer in Dietrich's seat. Rose never regained it and Meyer later rowed in the bow at the 1964 Olympics. Dietrich never got to the Olympics.

At his engineering job Rose had been urged by a drafting associate to do something different. See the world. Go to the United States. Then at the suggestion of a Ratzeburg friend, Dietrich wrote to Jack Kelly in Philadelphia asking what it might take to join Vesper. Kelly quickly responded and soon Rose was on his way.

The friend was the six man in the Ratzeburg eight, Karl Von Groddeck, a mountain of a man, a journalist by trade and an elite rower by choice. Rose tells this story. Von Groddeck earlier had belonged to a rowing club in Hamburg, as did Rose, and at a regatta one time the coach ordered Von Groddeck to drop down to lesser senior eight for a race in which he hoped to add some easy point to the club's total.

Von Groddeck was incensed and threatened to throw overboard any trophy that might be won as a result. His crew did win and Von Groddeck did throw the trophy in the drink, before a shocked hometown crowd of 5,000. Of course he was too was thrown, not in the water but out of the club. He then went to row with the Ratzeburg group along with Dietrich who in a few years went on to America.

With the Kelly invitation and travel funds, Rose reached New York by ship and took a train to Philadelphia where Kelly met him at the 30th street station. Jack was on his way first to an interview at the studio of WCAU-TV and then to lunch at a country club. Kelly helped carry Dietrich's wooden suitcase, commenting on how much it weighed. Rose in turn was impressed with the importance of Kelly and the buffet at the club. "I never saw so much food in my life. You could eat whatever you wanted and there was so much of it."

Dietrich made his home in the well-used attic of the Vesper boat house and set about getting work. Kelly introduced him to Bill Knecht who had a need for engineers. But the fit was not professionally right and together they found the perfect job for Rose with a duct-work design company of Paul Yoman's, where he worked for 11 years.

Rose was unimpressed with the Vesper boat house. By European standards it was small and by orderly German standards its equipment not properly maintained. Also no one was around.

"Where are the oarsmen," Rose asked. Kelly explained they were rowing at the Pan American games in South America. "Be patient," said Jack. "Row in a single. People will soon be coming back."

The Vespers did come back but fewer than those who went. Many quit the sport after a disappointing effort in the Pan Am games. After Kelly dismissed the coach, Tibor Macan, it was his thought that perhaps Rose could become a coach while all Dietrich had in mind was to row.

Dietrich Rose played a major role in the upcoming success of Vesper, the spark that ignited the club in 1963. He was quickly elected by his peers to be the Vesper captain and he introduced a strenuous off-the-water weightlifting and conditioning program. Also he reinforced and added to Allen Rosenberg's thoughts on training and rigging.

Because he saw his role as an oarsman, and neither a coach nor a trainer, he did everything side by side with the candidates for the Vesper boats. He said, "I was impressed at how strong the American oarsmen were, much stronger than their European counterparts. Once Vesper learned the training routine and did the weight lifting the oarsmen naturally surpassed what was being done in Ratzeburg."

Dietrich quickly picked up the English language and I do not recall any misunderstanding in what he wanted from us. Nothing seemed daunting for him and he was the cheerleader that Rosenberg simply was not. His spirit and enthusiasm were contagious. While disappointed, he understood his lack of American citizenship would keep him off the highest of American teams for international competition.

Dietrich Rose on his bicycle advising Stroke Bill Stowe and coxswain Bob Zimonyi on the finer points of carrying the shell.

Apart from that, Dietrich was not as smooth and skilled an oarsman as is necessary for success on the highest level. His free-for-all style when under racing pressure was as big an obstacle as his lack of citizenship. But Dietrich Rose was a part of the team effort, his contribution just as important to our effort as that of anyone in the Vesper Olympic eight. Maybe more so.

9

Young Hugh Foley Shows Up

Early in the summer of 1963 the youngest and least experienced member of what became the Olympic eight walked into the Vesper boat house. In no way recruited, or even spotted casually for his potential, Hugh Foley arrived for a good sport experience. He was our first undergraduate oarsman, one never imagining that in a year he would be sitting in the unquestioned fastest shell in the world.

Foley was born in March, 1944, in Seattle, Washington, but spent most of his youth in Martin City, Montana, where his father was a logger and forester turned farmer. He had no idea that rowing existed, nor did he harbor any Olympic aspirations. Hugh was a fair athlete who competed in football, basketball and track at a small high school on the fringes of the Glacier National Park with a graduating class of sixty.

Hugh's mother, a good Catholic, wanted him to go to parochial school but had agreed that if he went to a Catholic college, he did not have to attend the nearest church school for his secondary education. Foley applied to three Catholic colleges on the West Coast and decided on Loyola in Los Angeles. Why?

He said, "I was watching pro football, the Rams playing in the Los Angeles Coliseum, on our only television station and I saw everyone sitting in the stadium in shirt sleeves. At the time we had snow up to the second pane of glass on the first floor window. So I decided Los Angeles was for me. Late in the summer of 1962, I boarded the train to Portland, Oregon, and then on to Los Angeles, where this hayseed got on a city bus with a suitcase and a trunk for the final leg to the university.

"Several of my new college friends encouraged me to participate in their favorite pastimes, one surfing and the other crew. On the morning I had committed to try both, the surfer slept in. Or I might today be a surfboard bum. I soon found myself at the Marina Del Rey where there was nothing at the time except a gas station and a very crude boathouse. John McHugh, a transplanted Philadelphia engineer, was the Loyola freshman coach and we suffered through a mediocre season.

"The one race experience that stands out in my memory was my stroking the frosh boat in a race against the University of Southern California. Just before the start a tug boat crept up behind us and blasted its whistle to signal a bridge opening. We took off at the first toot, rowing higher than ever before and won in an upset.

"John McHugh encouraged several of us to travel to Philadelphia and gain some real racing experience as most of the serious club rowing was on the East Coast. Jim Campbell had rowed for Vesper the previous summer and liked it. So we took off in a car belonging to Dick Toby, another teammate, and eventually got to Vesper. Jack Kelly was generous and allowed us to stay at the Philadelphia Athletic Club where he apparently had an ownership position."

Foley was queried about his strengths and rowing qualifications. He said, "The best thing I had going for me was that I had grown up on a farm. When there was work to be done, you just did it. It had to be done, then and there."

With that rural farm boy background, Foley was always fit. He was not an immediate star for Vesper but his work ethic put him above the average and his anatomy, 6 foot 3, 190 pounds, helped him be recognized. Whatever merit and recognition he achieved at the club he earned, because he was not of the old guard nor did he arrive with any strong college or club credentials.

Foley kept to himself much of the time and was a bit of a mystery. Whether it was shyness or lack of confidence no one is sure. But he gained a reputation as being a steady, hard and uncomplaining worker, willing to dedicate himself to team goals. As the youngest man in a crowd of venerable characters, he always feared being the one who might first be cut in any selection process.

On August 10, 1963, Hugh stroked a Vesper four-with-cox in the Schuylkill Navy match race against Fairmont Boat Club. Jim Campbell, his Loyola teammate, was his three man. Records were not kept of these fun Saturday morning developmental races so no one recalls the winner. But the three man in the Fairmont four was Stan Cwiklinski who would become the three man of Vesper's 1964 Olympic eight.

Foley catapulted into prominence when he rowed in the two seat for the Vesper eight that unexpectedly won the Middle States Regatta on September 1, 1963. That victory qualified this crew to represent the U.S. at the Tokyo International Sports Festival to be held in mid-October, an experience explained in the following chapter.

By then Foley had no intention of returning to Los Angeles and Loyola. With the help of John McHugh, he transferred his credits and entered LaSalle College in Philadelphia.

I always had confidence in Hugh's willingness to give his all. When the coxswain commanded, "All Together," I knew that Hugh Foley would answer the call as a full member of our racing machine.

10

Tokyo Sports Festival

A year before the 1964 Olympic games the Tokyo organizing committee staged a rehearsal with athletes from around the world invited to participate in mid-October. For the crew races the squads from West Germany and the United States would row over the reconstructed 2,000-meter Toda rowing course, the one built in 1930 and never used for the 1940 Olympics called off due to World War II.

The National Association of Amateur Oarsmen, the outfit that selected and certified U.S. rowing participants for international competition, determined that the American team would be chosen on the basis of results of the Middle States Regatta on Philadelphia's Schuylkill River on September 1. Those selected had to prove that they could effectively row in the small boats, the fours and pairs, as well as in eights.

Vesper's eight had been beaten three times, at the U.S. championships, the Independence Day and the Schuylkill Navy regattas. Because the proposed trip came during the academic year few collegians would be competing. The clubs, like the Lake Washington Rowing Club of Seattle featuring the Olympian and rowing tourist Ted Nash, would predominate.

Thanks to some fancy shuffling of the lineup by coach Rosenberg the Vesper eight won a qualifying race by a length and a quarter over the favored Lake Washington/Riverside combination boat as well as entries from the Potomac and the College boat clubs.

The Vesper eight included five future Olympians: Joe and Tom Amlong, Hugh Foley, Bill Knecht and coxswain Bob Zimonyi. The others were the Vesper captain Dietrich Rose, Walt Birbeck and the Flanigan twins, Dick and Don.

The victory was unexpected as was the performance of the Amlong brothers whose prior efforts left much to be desired. Rowing as a pair in the Middle States Regatta they upset the national champions from the Potomac Boat Club, Jim Edmonds and Tony Johnson, by a comfortable three seconds with a blazing finish in the last quarter mile.

The third qualifying race for the fours was a confusing scramble and had to be rowed twice following a steering incident and the disqualification of the Potomac entry. The Ted Nash four from Lake Washington/Riverside was the victor but that was not enough to outweigh Vesper's triumphs among the eights and the pairs. So the N.A.A.O officials picked the Vesper group for the Tokyo trip.

Sean Shea, a small but skilled and determined Philadelphian was named to replace Don Flanigan who had just been accepted to Hahnemann Hospital Medical School in Philadelphia. This caused a furor and was the first of many Vesper confrontations with Jack Sulger, president of the N.A.A.O. and the rowing impresario of the influential New York Athletic Club.

Sulger contended the changed boat that had won the Middle States qualifier was no longer the true U.S. representative and perhaps the second-place eight was now faster. It was too late to find out and thus the men of Vesper prepared for the Trans Pacific voyage. The contingent consisted of just eight oarsmen, one coxswain and one coach, Rosenberg. No spares.

I need to say something about the Flanigans. The 6-foot 4 twins were smooth and effective oarsmen in pairs or fours but perhaps not quite as gritty and strong as some of the newcomers in the Vesper boat house. They had also rowed at St. Joseph's College where their rookie coach had been Allen Rosenberg whom they praised unilaterally.

However the Amlong brothers were merciless in criticism of the Flanigans, possibly because the twins had once beaten them in a national championship pair-without-coxswain event. Dick Flanigan had a generous comment. He said years later, "The Amlongs were arrogant and rough around the edges, always irritating, generally obnoxious. But they have mellowed with old age. I have met them at masters races and they were not too bad—both with kind and nice wives."

Don Flanigan had a story. He said that way back during the remodeling of the Vesper boat house two urinals were installed in the locker room appropriately named Joe and Tom with plaques above them. This won approval of the many Vesper oarsmen who had been tarnished by comments of the brothers from Virginia. Those urinals became their regular chance to piss on Joe and Tom.

In the next year, as preparation for the Olympic trials continued, Dick and Don were always helpful to us around the boat house, reinforcing our ambitions.

Once in Tokyo it was determined that the United States and German crews would row three events against the champions of Nippon—pairs and fours without coxswains and the eights. Joe and Tom would row in all three, joining Bill Knecht and Dietrich Rose in the four.

The Vesper flight to Tokyo, via Chicago, San Francisco and Honolulu, took 26 hours. For Foley that was his first time aboard an airplane! The group settled into the new luxurious Dai-Ichi Hotel, joining 600 athletes from around the world. The rowing course was an hour from the hotel and the Vesper oarsmen would take along box lunches so as to stay at the course for a second afternoon workout.

The group was advised that each event would have preliminary heats and the schedule made it impossible for the Amlongs to row in the four with Knecht and Rose. Their replacements were Dick Flanigan and Foley forming a new combination without any practice together.

An eight-oared shell had earlier been sent to Tokyo by the University of Pennsylvania and it was quickly rigged and easily adjusted to suit the crew. On the other hand the small boats to be used were local ones called Deltas and generally built for the smaller Japanese men. These shells took some major rigging adjustments, such as elevating and extending the slides and removing the rudders. Dietrich Rose proved his worth with his skill in re-rigging those lightweight boats.

In the initial heats the Amlongs cruised to an easy victory. The U.S. four recovered from steering problems to qualify for the final too with a confidence-building time equal to that of the favored West Germans. The result in the final for the pairs was gold medals for Joe and Tom, winners by six lengths over the West German pair, the European champions of 1959.

Rosenberg recalled that the final for the fours the next day was a magnificent race, the U.S. entry second to West Germany by just half a second. The Germans recovered after steering into a buoy and won on the last stroke with their cadence at the end 46 strokes a minute.

The slow time of 6 minutes, 40 seconds for former and future West German Olympians Meyer, VonGroddeck, Behrens and Bittner reflected the borrowed boat and a steady headwind. Foley stroked a fine race and surged from a deficit of two lengths at 500 meters to a near triumph in the time of 6:40.5.

Vesper thus proved it had the skills of watermen under adverse climactic conditions and that bode well for the club's future. So, too, for the eight in its event that followed against the famous Ratzeburg crew representing West Germany.

Since I was not there I have relied on Rosenberg's account. Allen said, "Monday's race in the eights was punctuated by false starts by the Japanese and German crews. On the third effort the race was on. Germany took the lead at the outset and at 400 meters had more than a one boat length advantage rowing at a 43 strokes per minute. The United States faltered briefly after a good start and, at

36, started to move at 1000 meters. At 1500 meters there was no open water and we were still moving on them. We finished in 6:21, two-thirds of a boat length behind Ratzeburg which finished in a slow time of 6:19.5. Dietrich Rose stroked a great race against his old German clubmates."

Sean Shea had rowed himself into unconsciousness and was taken out of the boat by Japanese Naval scuba divers. Shea recovered quickly but as part of the drill he was whisked off to a hospital in a dramatic departure.

For many in the Vesper crew this race amounted to a world-class championship, one that took all their concentration and strength to do as well as they did. Doing that well against the 1960 Olympic champions was a huge confidence builder, especially for a novice like Foley. While the race was televised and covered by news services all over Europe and the Far East, its importance was overlooked in the U.S.

For a veteran of international races like Bill Knecht this occasion had been a chance to sightsee. The race was really not all that important. Similarly the Ratzeburg oarsmen considered this a wonderful extracurricular boondoggle. They had treated their American tour the previous spring in the same manner—win but don't show all your stuff.

Rowing in Tokyo gave Rosenberg and Rose the opportunity to study the rowing course which proved invaluable a year later. For the most part the European rowing courses are laid out to take advantage of prevailing tailwinds and the Ratzeburg style of rowing is short in the water and a high stroking cadence, both advantageous with a tailwind. However, the Toda course did not seem to have a prevailing wind and headwinds were not uncommon. This early knowledge of the anticipated conditions for 1964 helped Vesper to design both a crew and a style that could present an advantage over the Germans on that knowledge alone.

Following the races both the American and German contingents participated in a series of physiological experiments and telemetric tests conducted by Dr. Ishiko of the Tokyo School of Medicine. The Germans showed that they were vastly stronger than the Americans as well as other competitors. One of the tests was to measure lung capacity and absorption of oxygen, and it crudely consisted of the athletes holding their breath as long as they could. Dietrich Rose demonstrated his worth by holding his breath until unconscious. He collapsed, hit his head on his fall and required medical attention and stitches.

After all this the athletes were given a restful recovery trip to the mountain area of Nikko and several days of sightseeing and shopping in Tokyo which was the real lure of the trip for the veterans of sports tourism. This was not understood by the younger athletes who came to prove themselves athletically. While some went home with pearls and trinkets, Hugh Foley returned to the United States with the naive yet useful conviction that the Germans could be beaten.

11

Two Yale Guys Show Up

While the best of the Vesper talent was in Tokyo on the rowing boondoggle, two more key players established themselves in Philadelphia to train for the Olympics. This naive duo came unrecruited by Kelly; they had no boat nor a club and were without any idea how to accomplish their intention which was to make the 1964 Olympic Team in a pair. Their motivation was to avenge injustices they felt they had suffered in their years rowing for Yale.

I have wished to treat the nine characters in the Vesper eight as the great individuals they were and still are. However Boyce Budd and Emory Clark, like the Amlong brothers, are so interlinked as a twosome that they blend and almost lose their personal identities. So I bring them along together as the best seats in the Vesper engine room.

The older is Emory Clark, born in Detroit on March 23, 1938. Clark first held an oar as an eighth grader at Groton, one of the toney New England prep schools with the acronym St. Grottlesex. He and a classmate were permitted to take an old heavy wooden lapstrake training boat out on the green, putrid Nashua River. There they had fun. Clark then rowed in the Groton intramural boats and by his junior and senior years he had made the first four-with-cox, the school's varsity boat of choice. In his senior or sixth-form year John Higginson, later to row for Harvard, was the captain.

Clark entered Yale in the fall of 1956 and immediately was influenced by the Yale varsity eight which had won the U.S. Olympic trials and was in training for the games. That crew was the winner at Melbourne in late November. This was heady stuff for a college freshman who started off on the right foot at Yale by winning a place in an undefeated freshman boat.

As a sophomore he easily made the Yale varsity which had in it two Olympic gold medal winners, John Cooke and Rusty Wailes. Emory could even see himself as an Olympian in 1960, his graduation year, if things went right. But they went wrong. The coach, Jim Rathschmidt, became ill and the crew lost momentum. Clark was voted captain for his senior year and his crew did not win a single race—a depressing disaster for a young man who so loved the sport. College rowing left Emory with an awful taste.

Although he excelled at rowing Clark never considered himself much of an athlete. His size, 6-4, 200, well qualified him for crew but he was awkward, gangly, without much grace or coordination. I always thought he walked like a duck.

Years later Allen Rosenberg told me that Clark had hammer toes which caused his unusual gait but had nothing to do with his effectiveness sitting down in a boat. I too was a rough stylist and I always felt better when around Emory because in comparison he made me look good. He claimed to adore football, which he played at Groton, and told me, "I loved bumping into people."

After his discouraging senior year at Yale, Clark joined the Marines, was commissioned and sent to the Orient with few thoughts of ever rowing again. Then here came Boyce Budd who had an even more discouraging experience at Yale.

Budd, one class behind Clark rowed in a poor freshman boat, made the varsity as a sophomore and then was demoted to the second varsity for his junior and senior years. Ouch! He had been an average high school athlete in New Jersey, and did a postgraduate year at a prep school, Lawrenceville, before entering Yale. After he was cut from the freshman football squad the coaches grabbed him for crew, of which he knew nothing, because of his size and raw potential. Like Emory, he was in awe of Yale's 1956 Olympic Crew.

Other Olympic seeds were planted when, after graduation, he went to England for a year of study at Cambridge. He rowed there in the famous Boat Race against Oxford, the annual springtime rite over four miles, 374 yards on The Thames and which dates back to 1829. Boyce helped Cambridge win that year.

While training with the Cambridge group Boyce met John Lecky, a skilled oarsman from Canada also in England for post graduate studies. They rowed together in a pair at Henley and Boyce's ambitions were hatched in the incubator of enthusiasm created by his close friendship with Lecky. With Lecky, Boyce smoothed over much of his animal roughness that held him back at Yale.

Budd and Clark corresponded regularly and they dared to think about making an Olympic effort. In a November 1, 1962 letter from Boyce in New Jersey to Clark with the Marines in the Pacific the rough plans were laid out for their eventual partnership and its training program. I quote much of this letter because it expresses so well the enthusiastic zeal that the Yale duo contained and eventually brought to Vesper.

"Dear Em: Well buddy, I know what a bastard I've been not to answer the letter you sent me in Ireland but it ain't like I've been ignoring that letter ever since I received it. You might be interested to know that I have been doing a considerable amount of thinking and some limited research in the field of rowing here in the United States and I have some big news to tell you about. Now for one thing, I have decided that come hell or high water, I for one am going to be participating in the 1964 Olympic trials and I hope rowing in Tokyo.

"Em, I am now a Marine. I have joined a reserve unit here in New Jersey and am probably going away to Paris Island in January. We have big things to talk about. I'm certain for one thing that we can row for the Marines. A big rowing club is starting in New York and the trials in 1964 are going to be held at Pelham Bay on a new man-made course that the City of New York is building. By then I probably will be working in New York and will thus be close to those facilities. I have spoken to The Rath (referring to Yale coach Jim Rathschmidt) and he is very enthusiastic about the idea of you and me in a pair-with.

"Em, I could not be more enthusiastic about anything than I am about this and I sincerely hope that you and I can team up in a pair and win the whole lot. I am willing to lose a job and willing to spend any amount of time and energy to gain this and I intend to train like I have never trained before. Of course this will involve more severe training than you and I have ever done before but I'm sure that we can drive each other on better than most people can. I must tell you that I have some very specific ideas about training for a pair with which The Rath has agreed completely.

"Before I go on, you should know that those two German boys that John (Lecky) and I might have beaten are the world champions in the pair with, having beaten the pants off the American pair. The Germans won five of the seven events at Lucerne.

"My suggestion for a training program would involve a prodigious amount of running (up hills especially), a program of lifting weights, fairly light ones where the exercise is repeated many times, and much playing of games such as squash or handball to turn two elephantine lardasses like ourselves into agile oarsmen. Also I think that almost before we touch a pair that we ought to learn to row a single scull. I can manage one now but I know from experience that if you can manage a single then you have a much easier time handling a pair. They are both very tricky boats to row well. I think that you should get your rowing technique back by finding a single and training in that because we will both be very depressed when we step into a pair and find that we are rowing like two five-year old kids, and are not gold medalists right off the bat.

"The small boat trials are going to be held in August of 1964 and consequently I think that we must start training as soon as I get out of the Marines in July of 1963. Now we should be running, weightlifting and rowing lightly all through the winter, starting the really serious work in April (1963). I realize how long this sounds but I know what this international competition is like and if we feel like being in their league at all it is going to take an extraordinary effort.

"By the way, John and I used some of the German interval training methods and I would like to do that again if you agree. I'm afraid that 28 strokes a minute won't do. We are going to have to hump that pair-with along at about 33 to 35 in the body of the race if we hope to be in striking distance, but that is no problem we will find.

"Problems: how to get you stationed in or near New York from next summer to go to the trials; how to get the Marines to pay for part of the cost of our training program; where to get a really fine boat and the proper oars? The Rath would be glad to do some coaching and there are plenty of places to row, and he will write for you to the Marines. Could you get stationed near here? With a will and the kind of devotion that it will take, you and I could win two gold medals. Write to me and tell me what you think of this. We must start now! What do you think, Buddy? Boyce."

This letter really started the process for the Yale duo and the wisdom of the training methods detailed by Boyce was extraordinary for 1962. Logistical details had to be worked out and since Clark was not to be released from the Marines until May of 1964, special orders had to be secured in order to train on the East Coast. He sent a request for transfer on February 1, 1963, but that got caught up in government bureaucracy and nothing happened.

By the time he sent in second request, July 1963, he was stationed in Camp Pendleton, California. At last on August 1, 1963 he received orders to report to the Marine Corps supply center in Philadelphia, and he reported in September 3, 1963. While this was not the requested New York or New Haven, Clark reasoned as he wrote afterward, "You take what they give you. The idea of Jim Rathschmidt coaching us (at Yale) went by the board. Thank God for that for, while I didn't know it, Philadelphia and more particularly the Vesper Boat Club were to become the center of the U.S. rowing effort in 1964. Those orders to the Marine Supply Activity were the first of a series of miraculous coincidences which were to comprise the Cinderella story of the 1964 Vesper eight."

Stories regarding the entrance of Budd and Clark at Vesper vary according to the teller and Rosenberg recalls their arriving at the door looking for a pair to row, the one over at the Fairmont Boat Club being too small for their bulk. Allen says he of course welcomed these promising giants, that the marriage was done.

Others have said that Budd and Clark wanted to be coached by the renowned Joe Burk at the University of Pennsylvania but Burk was too busy and referred them to Vesper. I must to go with Emory's following description of his hapless arrival at 10 Boathouse Row, the home of Vesper.

"Upon arrival in Philadelphia I called John Carlin, the North American representative to FISA (the international governing body of rowing), introduced myself, and told him I needed a single scull to start training. He was very kind, suggesting that I come down to his club, Fairmont, on the weekend and he would see what he could do. Thanking him, I hung up and called Dave Wilmerding, bowman of the 1957 Yale Varsity, who immediately understood my urgency, promised to contact Jack Kelly, Vesper's patron saint, and told me to be at Vesper at 5:30 that afternoon. I showed up and Wilmerding, true to his word, had arranged with Kelly for me to use a single. I rowed my first wobbly training mile of the Schuylkill that evening. That row was the beginning of thirteen months of training during which I rowed twice a day, six days a week, and lifted or ran each night after the workout on the river."

Unlike the Rosenberg recall of greeting the Yale pair with open arms, Emory has said, "About the third day of rowing out of Vesper I was accosted by a vitriolic little buzz saw who proceeded to denounce college oarsmen in general, and me in particular, for having no respect for the club rowing, claiming we merely wanted to use club equipment and facilities without contributing anything. In any case Allen Rosenberg, for that is who it was, always felt very strongly about whatever position he was espousing and was never long on diplomacy.

"A former coxswain who was Kelly's designated Vesper coach at the time, Allen was living in the boathouse apartment. I did not then imagine he would become a pivotal figure in our effort and would become a close friend. When he left with a Vesper eight for a pre-Olympic regatta and Boyce arrived early in October we had the boat house as well as the river to ourselves."

Sportswriters and commentators overuse words like focus, determination, and commitment. Athletes don't care for this verbiage describing their routes to success, but these words do assert the actions of Budd and Emory as they plodded on. Others, like me, simply rowed from day to day hoping for the best, first to get in shape, next to make a boat go fast and then to gain the confidence of others within the boat. If we might win a race, all the better.

But Boyce and Emory had a single purpose, and that was to win at the Olympics. Their diets, off-water training, mindset, everything else, was funneled to this goal which they actually expected to achieve.

12

Philadelphia's Native Son, Stan Cwiklinski

Stan Cwiklinski, whose last name we could hardly pronounce let alone spell, was the only one of us in the final Vesper Olympic eight native to Philadelphia—the only one with a sense of that city's grit and the Schuylkill's quirks.

It was our fortune that he came into Vesper by the suggestion of Hugh Foley, the recent Montana transfer to LaSalle College where Hugh found Cwiklinski as a classmate. This was in that key winter of 1963-64.

Of course Allen Rosenberg takes claim for the capture of Stan. He remembers seeing this 6-foot 3, 190 pound blond Polish kid row by, having come out of the Fairmount Boat Club. When Stan returned, Rosenberg was there inviting him to join Vesper's Olympic campaign. This is the way it should have been, but only Al remembers it that way.

There was a problem on the Schuylkill's Boathouse Row with regard to "club jumping." It was not proper for the coach of one club to lure an oarsman from another. Perhaps Rosenberg, admiring Stan's potential sills and appearance, went around a corner by suggesting to Foley that he conveniently bump into Cwiklinski, the LaSalle classmate, and extend an invitation to come over for a row at Vesper in a casual mannerly way. On Boathouse Row an indirect approach was deemed an acceptable method of filching another club's rowing talent.

It has been said that Foley, in the LaSalle student union cafeteria, struck up a conversation with his target, Cwiklinski, and dropped the invitation. Good enough that this powerful young, athlete boarded our Olympic train at the right time.

Stan once pointed out to me that the artist Thomas Eakins, the splendid painter of the 19th century Schuylkill rowing scene, was born in 1843, 100 years before he was born, a fact of huge importance to Stan. Eakins had also attended Stan's Philadelphia high school, Central by name.

Stan had backed into rowing. Once upon a Sunday afternoon walk with his father into the city's Fairmount Park they had peeked in the windows of the clubs along Boathouse Row. What he saw remained mysterious.

Central High had no crew but a varsity football team of course and also a fencing one and Stan belonged to both. He was a state champion in epee. Those sports took care of autumn and winter and to fulfill the spring gap a classmate, Rod Berry, suggested a daily commute over to the Fairmount Boat Club where they could scull together. That was fortuitous.

Stan had played football for Central when it somehow won the city public school championship with a team of intelligent, studious players. Central was comparable to New York City's Stuyvesant or Bronx High School of Science, full of bright Jewish kids not known for athletic abilities or big bodies. Little Al Rosenberg had been an athlete of sorts at Central.

Stan's team had earned the right to play the Catholic high school champions, Monsignor Bonner, for the Philadelphia city championship and the bragging rights. It proved to be a dubious privilege as Stan and his teammates were beaten up and humiliated, 52-0. That football game ended any thoughts Cwiklinski might have entertained about continuing contact sports or having a college football experience. Rowing took on new importance.

At Fairmount this neophyte was coached by a man named Frank Silvo, to whom Stan attributes his considerable motivation and eventual success. After floundering about in the beginning, as do all oarsmen, Stan won a high school championship on the Schuylkill in 1961, rowing in the heavyweight double scull class.

Then came college. Cwiklinski had instant success in the LaSalle freshman eight which placed first at the annual Dad Vail regatta on the Schuylkill, the latter long regarded as the small-college national championship event. But the oarsmen in that boat were scattered around as sophomores and failed to regain the feeling of a well knit crew or its enthusiasm. For Stan the experience of rowing in the 1962 varsity was neither fun nor successful.

His first exposure to a world class crew had come in the summer of 1961 when the Lake Washington Rowing Club's squad from Seattle settled into Fairmount to train for the national championships. These giants—at least in Stan's eyes—had won Olympic gold medals in the four-without-cox at Rome the summer before and they were an inspiration to a impressionable young oarsman.

In the summer of 1963 Stan was asked to row with the Schuylkill Navy composite boat, meaning its oarsmen were all-stars from the various Boathouse Row clubs. Olympic aspirations were in the air and Stan had some credentials.

The Vesper invitation came a few months later and it was a cold and windy December evening on the Schuylkill when Stan had his first row out of that boat house. He was sent out in a four with Boyce Budd, Emory Clark and Hugh Foley.

I can only imagine the dynamics between these two couples, the older, experienced Yale duo and two impressionable undergraduate kids from relatively insignificant LaSalle College. Regardless of what transpired the coach in the launch, Rosenberg, called Stan into his Vesper apartment afterward and said, "I liked what I saw tonight and I want you to keep coming down and rowing with us." The kid did so and further impressed the coach with his knowledge of the demands of weightlifting. Quiet and shy, Stan did what he was told.

Like Foley earlier, he feared that being the last man selected into this tight little group he might be the first one out—should someone better come along. But Stan realized too he was in the right place to earn a slot on next year's Olympic team, and he was willing to work diligently for that privilege.

Cwiklinski? It's pronounced quick-LIN-skee.

13

Bill Stowe Completes The Eight

Your author was the last of the final Vesper Olympic eight to arrive on the Philadelphia rowing scene. On grounds of modesty, false or otherwise, I call upon Emory Clark to fill in for this writer—to describe my role from the position of a Vesper teammate. These comments come from Clark's own memoir and he has some nice things to say about me, with the exception of my physical composition.

In recognizing the endeavors of Kelly and Rosenberg so far, Clark writes, "While the makeup of the final Tokyo eight was by no means yet arranged or even recognized, the pieces of the puzzle were assembling. Bill Stowe was the last piece.

"Bill was, and is, a blithe spirit. Outspoken in his likes and beliefs, he constantly unsettled his friends with his lack of hypocrisy, saying exactly what he felt when he felt it. His charm was he could do this without hurting people, as his kindness and magnanimity of spirit took away whatever sting might otherwise accompany his words. Conservative in philosophy but liberal in emotion, Bill appeared at the boathouse in March, 1964, I believe as a direct result of Jack Kelly's string pulling in Washington.

"He was a lieutenant junior grade in the Navy and arrived fresh from Saigon where, with his Cornell hotel school administration background, he had managed the American Officer's Club there—not an inconsiderable job in that war torn country which was poised on the threshold of a great influx of American military. To hear Bill tell it, and his stories were legion, all his job involved was orchestrating cocktail parties on the roof of the club while witnessing each coup as one corrupt regime followed another.

"In any case, he arrived in Philadelphia to row with the blessing of the U.S. Navy and, despite a large naval installation in south Philadelphia, he was not burdened with other tasks of an official nature. As far as I know when Bill was not on the water he was playing golf, working in a brokerage house, or relaxing—which he did very well. Despite his lack of physical training and considerable bulk, being one of those who quickly displays indulgence and who always looked as if he needed a brassiere, the stroke seat was his from the beginning. It amazed me how quickly he was able to go all out and how strong he was, particularly since I had a six months' training lead on him. Unlike some strokes, who are there for their spirit, their ability to pass the rhythm back and keep the stroke up, Bill pulled as much or more water than most six men."

In Clark's log for May 28, 1964, he had written, "Last night the eight began to move with Bill Stowe stroking. Boyce rode in the coach's launch cause of a crick in his back. But the damn boat really moved and for the first time I did some work and wasn't rushed. Lying in bed this morning I was getting excited about the eight. We could win everything with that boat if they'd just get organized and not be so damn haphazard. I liked Stowe at stroke and that I was at seven. The whole thing brought back great memories—an eight that can really move. Damn that excites me. Made the whole week worthwhile."

With Emory Clark's kind words recorded, I can now tell the painful, personal truth.

I was born exactly two years to the day after Emory. Raised in suburban New York and I had no knowledge of the sport of rowing until I was sent to prep school in Kent, Connecticut. As a youngster I had failed in every attempt at athletics, always being the last one chosen in the humiliating chose-up for any grade school recess team. Fly balls in Little League baseball fell painfully on my toes instead of in my mitt. I was raised in the shadow of an older brother who seemed to be good at every sport he chose. I could survive in the water but could hardly swim. Later in life I passed a rigorous Navy water survival course, but would fail any kind of a swimming test. I never had the courage to learn how to dive and even today I enter the water from the shallow end of a pool, under the guise that I don't like the shock of the cold water.

As a non-athlete, I was pathetic and was embarrassed to try anything. I was chubby and remember my wonderful mom taking me to the doctor to see if I had some internal gland problems that were making me fat.

At the Kent School I was further degraded as a poor student and my self esteem approached new lows. Being big and overweight, I played without distinction as a lineman on one of the intramural football teams. On the ice I slipped around while learning hockey and never knew how to stop my sliding mass. Failure loomed as my teammates moved ahead to varsity levels. I stayed back and shoveled the snow off the intramural hockey rink.

But the spring of 1955 brought me a new opportunity in a sport where no one was a natural and everyone started on the same footing. Rowing was huge at Kent. Varsity oarsmen were considered gods. They had three intramural clubs which raced one other with utmost competitiveness and it was always fun. Each club had at least three eight-oared shells afloat daily on the Housatonic River which went right by the campus. My first spring season I flailed away equally with other novices. I was seated in the third Macedonian eight and we won some races, over the Housatonics and the Algos. Those names derived from the valley, river and mountain where Kent School situates. I was no worse than the others in the boat and we had to be somewhat all together to move the 61-foot wooden eight. I was finally excited about a physically demanding sport and my older brother was one of the gods, rowing in the Kent second varsity boat.

With newfound determination, I worked hard toward making the first Macedonian eight as a sophomore. We won the club championship and the right to race against Yale University' s Berkeley College eight on a Wednesday afternoon in May, 1956. My coach was a wonderful man, Rugged Ralph Richie, whose primary job at Kent was to teach freshman year English. He had given me a chance by not failing me in his course, allowing me to stay with my peers, and I am eternally grateful to him.

Our boat was good and I was a respected part of a team, even though I was placed in the four seat, a repository for the worst oarsman in the boat. That was something I did not know and would not realize until I became a rowing coach some ten years later.

Our Macedonian Club eight defeated the Yale boat and I was on top of the world. Tote Walker, the varsity coach, had even let us use one of the newer boats after we promised that we would be careful not to run it aground in the winding river. I felt the whole world was focused on this important race, and we won it! Later in life I learned that the residential college or club rowing system at Yale was made up of former prep school oarsmen who did not want to make the effort required of earning a place on the varsity. They enjoyed their social life and did not take this race as seriously as my teammates and I. We were elated yet we went unnoticed by the rest of the world.

Also unnoticed was that I had outgrown some of my baby fat and had gained strength to match my pride in this new found sport. Of course my brother had rowed in the Kent varsity that raced at the Royal Henley Regatta in England. He went on to Dartmouth to be a part of rebuilding a crew program which had gone stale.

As a Kent junior I earned a seat in the second varsity boat and we went unde-feated after losing our season opener against Yale's lightweight junior varsity eight. Heady stuff. I was still in the four seat and glad to be there. This was the big time as schoolboy rowing went. Our coach was Tote Walker, a former Yale coxswain, a geometry teacher, and the executive secretary of the Kent Alumni Association—a magnificent person to whom I owe my success as an oarsman and person.

In his retirement he continued to help me with rowing problems and I would regularly write Tote and his wife newsy letters about rowing. At the age of 95 he suggested that I write a book—about anything—because he so enjoyed hearing from me. That's why this writing effort is dedicated to Tote Walker, a wonderful man we respected and loved.

By senior year I had gained confidence in myself and was given a position of responsibility as an officer of the student body. Kent being a school with Episco-pal roots, church life was important and I was named the Sacristan of the Chapel to the surprise of anyone who knew me. I concentrated on the rowing and I made the varsity eight, albeit at the least skillful positions of two or four. Our crew was good, and like my brother's team two years before, we earned the right to go to Henley.

Before my last rowing season, college applications had to be processed and submitted. I applied to three universities with strong rowing programs and mak-ing certain none had foreign language requirements for graduation. To my huge surprise, I was accepted at the University of Pennsylvania, Syracuse, and Cornell. In the 1950's the best rowing program was at Cornell, so I accepted the opportu-nity to attend its famous School of Hotel Administration, which offered no threat to me of a ruinous foreign language requirement. Besides New York State law permitted 18-year olds to drink beer which wasn't true in Pennsylvania. That eliminated Penn from my consideration even though it had a fabulous crew coach in Joe Burk.

In June of 1958 our Kent crew was off to row in England aboard the magnifi-cent Queen Mary. We took several hydraulic rowing machines and practiced sev-eral times daily on deck. Our shell was hung thwartships in the ship's crew's drinking lounge, "The Pig & Whistle." Daily we would venture below to check our fragile boat which was too near the darts-playing area for our comfort.

At Henley the crews race in pairs on the narrow course with the loser elimi-nated and the winner advancing, like a tennis tournament. The match-ups are supposedly drawn at random from the pool of regatta entrants. We suffered elim-ination from the Harvard lightweight varsity, a defeat which set up for me a lifetime dislike for anything, if not everybody, to do with Harvard. We took consolation in that we gave them their closest race, as they went on to win the Thames Cup.

Afterward Tote Walker gave me superb advice when I asked him what he thought about my chances to row at Cornell. He said, "Don't tell them you ever rowed before and don't talk about your experiences. They will know and they will respect you for your silence. Also, start with the basics and don't grouse about rowing with novices." He was right because the know-it-all prep school oarsmen did not last and were disliked by the huge raw-material novice boys that came out for a new sport they could grow into as had I.

Carl Ullrich, Cornell's freshman rowing coach, gave me the position of stroke in the fall rowing. This meant that I was the pacesetter of the crew, sort of like a quarterback. There are no stars in crew, yet the coxswain and the stroke are often distinguished from the others. The rest of the eight would follow the cadence that I set. It was a leadership role that I was happy to accept even though I felt a big responsibility. Best of all it was a boost of pride I needed.

The 1959 Cornell freshman crew was an awesome boat, one of the best I ever rowed for. We were undefeated, never threatened in any race. The few practices that we took with the varsity and second varsity proved disheartening to them because we could beat them.

We decided to try for a freshman record in the Intercollegiate Rowing Association (I.R.A.) national championship regatta that ended the collegiate rowing season. Going against 15 of the top freshman eights over a two-mile course on Syracuse's Onondaga Lake, we had a two-length lead over the next boat at the half-mile mark, four lengths at the halfway point and more than six lengths with half a mile remaining. No crew had ever taken such a lead at the I.R.A.—and remember that was over just the second-place crew with the other thirteen strung out farther behind.

I guess we pushed the boat a bit too hard because just after the mile and a half mark, our two man passed out and simply stopped rowing. The boat lurched a bit and I somehow said to John Abele, my seven man, "I guess we will just have to do it without Bob." The crowd went wild at the finish line because the pack was catching up and it might be close at the end. It wasn't though. We limped home more than two lengths ahead of the runner-up and became national champions.

Cornell oarsmen Bill Stowe and John Abele later rowed with Bob Zimonyi
Coxswain for Vesper Boat Club in the pair with cox.

It was a tradition that the winning boat be honored by rowing back to the finish-line dock first to the applause of the crowd. But our three man was out of it too and the five man was throwing up. If we were going to be the first crew to the dock it was up to farm-bred John Abele and myself to pretty much row the boat for about a half a mile. Having been in strict training since February, I could smell the beer from the college reunion tents along the shore and was determined to get to the dock fast.

With new found strength we horsed the boat in. I jumped out, asking someone else to collect the betting shirts we had won off the backs of our defeated rivals, and headed for a frosty brew. My behavior was not typical of Cornell oarsmen but I was unconcerned. We were the only Big Red boat to win that afternoon.

In the fall of sophomore year I arrived at the boathouse to work my way into the varsity eight. To my surprise I immediately assumed the position as stroke of that boat. I had a bad case of sophomore-itis, and got caught up in the party life after the fall training was over. A fraternity Christmas party became my undoing. After an afternoon of pre-party beer drinking, several buddies and I decided to bring one of the 'holy cows' into the frat house. We pinched it from the crèche in front of the Presbyterian Church in downtown Ithaca. The cow was such a hit at our party that we decided to return for the wonderful life-size king—or was it a wise man?—from the same nativity scene. This stupid mistake was later enhanced by the removal also of the baby Jesus to our Psi Upsilon House. All these figures were destroyed during the bash of a rock and roll party. More than one coed was seen leaving the party in tears over our sacrilege.

The evening activity cost me the spring rowing season since I was placed on social probation which made me ineligible for any intercollegiate athletics. To my fraternity brothers social probation meant nothing since they were not in any major activity. For me it meant no more rowing until junior year. I tried every possible way to get reinstated but to no avail. Tippy Goes, then one of rowing's leading officials, said in the New York Times the loss of Bill Stowe cost Cornell the chance to represent the U.S. in the 1960 Olympic games to be held in Rome. That had never occurred to me.

The Naval Academy's varsity eight went to Italy and rowed at Castel Gandolfo where the Midshipmen disappointed the American rowing community by taking a miserable fifth in the eight-oared finals, the poorest showing of a U.S. crew at the modern Olympics.

Perhaps I was fortunate not to have rowed that season. The fellow who had passed out in the two seat in our I.R.A. freshman race took my place stroking the varsity. While Cornell had a good varsity season the boat did not fare well at the Olympic trials.

Over the summer, while working in San Francisco, I ran daily and mentally prepared myself to work my way back to the varsity stroke seat by the spring of 1961. I had to regain the respect of the others and the head coach, Stork Sanford. To my surprise coach Sanford put me in at stroke at the fall's first practice in the fall. We had a good season, taking second in the IRA's to California…and winning all our dual races.

In the spring of 1962, my senior season, we took second at the Eastern Sprints Regatta and then won the varsity race at the IRA regatta at Syracuse. We were respectable—national champions—and had good times at Cornell's Collyer Boathouse.

Rather than go to England and the Henley regatta we voted to stay at home and race a Soviet crew in a special Philadelphia race on Independence Day, a match given a lot of cold-war press. The Schuylkill River shoreline drew an estimated 100,000 people to watch the race and enjoy the fourth of July in Fairmount Park. It was said to be the largest crowd in history to witness a crew race.

Cornell's traditional rowing style was not very compatible against the higher stroking Europeans and we lost in our game try to represent college rowing, to reinstate it as best in the world. The eight from the Vesper Boat Club surprised by taking second with Cornell third and three other American club boats behind us.

The Soviet crew accepting their medals after winning the Independence Day Regatta over Vesper and Cornell in 1962. Notice Jack Kelly handing out congratulations, just over the head of the coxswain.

"Who the hell is Vesper?" we asked ourselves, and I more loudly the rest.

There was another incident. Between the I.R.A. event in June and the Independence day regatta a decision was made to change Cornell's rowing trunks from a deep red color to pristine white. These new trunks outlined and projected the male genitals. I felt like I was wearing only underwear open to public gaze. Worse yet they stained easily and badly.

It was my routine to eat very lightly, if at all, the day of the race. I suppose I thought a hungry man was a mean man. Any prerace nervousness loosened my bowels, and I did not need that extra food. I could always be found in the toilet before a race taking what my teammates termed "nervous dumps." The prospect of racing the Russians put a special strain on me and just before we were to put our shell in the water at the University of Pennsylvania dock I felt an urge. But I was sure that nothing could remain in me and I took the chance that it was only gas to be vented. Very wrong. Our crew, anxious to get on the water, had to wait while I rinsed out those damn white shorts in the locker room. I rowed in wet but clean rowing trunks.

Having rowed in a national championship crew gave me many proud thoughts that have endured. Also we had overcome the so-called Sports Illustrated jinx by winning at Syracuse after our crew's photograph was on the cover of the magazine just before the I.R.A. regatta. That was supposed to be the kiss of death.

Then came a big change for me, entirely new adventures. I assumed my rowing days were over when I entered the U.S. Navy's officers candidate school and committed to a tour of three years and four months. The Navy officer who gave out assignments failed to convince me that I should sign up for destroyer duty. Rather I sought a position in Mess Management running one of those wonderful officers' clubs, a choice as promised by my enlistment. That officer, possibly resentful, gave me the worst assignment he could find, Vietnam. After attending a survival school in California, I was to report to Headquarters Support Activity, Saigon. I went to the library of the Newport officers school in Rhode Island to find the location of the Republic of Vietnam since I never heard of it. The atlas was old and had no Vietnam, only Indochina, and so I departed for this duty having no idea where I was going.

Exciting it was. On my first night in Saigon I went to the bar on the roof of the Majestic Hotel. There I pretended to be Humphrey Bogart under the ceiling fans of Rick's in Casablanca. From that lofty perch on the sixth floor overlooking the Mekong Delta and the Saigon River, I spotted several single shells being rowed amid the sampans and berthed warships. Observing them while sipping my Singapore Sling, I watched where the boathouse was located. The next day I signed up and became the only Occidental rowing member at the Club Nautique de Saigon. It proved to be great fun, but hardly resembling my Cornell experience.

The Club Nautique de Saigon rowing squad prior to departure for the Interport Regatta in Hong Kong, November 1963. The tall Occidental is author Bill Stowe.

The boats at the Club Nautique were old French-designed heavy lapstrake wherries and gigs. They were carried to and from the water by the club coolies. All the oarsman had to do upon arrival was to point to the boat desired. While you were dressing in the club white uniform in the locker room, the boat was readied for your use at waterside.

A club rule commanded one to always row against the tidal current when departing the boathouse. Should something untoward happen, then boat and rower could float back to the club and safely recover. It was never explained what might be the upsetting circumstances. Being shot by the Viet Cong wasn't mentioned, and on several occasions, I recall sprinting to get away from what looked like a suspect sampan.

The Club Nautique was less known for its rowing than for its wonderful French cuisine served on the patio overlooking the river. In Saigon I befriended several delightful Vietnamese and we had a good time, including racing in the Interport Regatta in Hong Kong. I became an official member of the five-person Vietnamese delegation there and had an instant bond with these club members.

Once an oarsman, always an oarsman wherever a rower might go. He or she will find instant camaraderie and fellow buffs wherever there's some suitable rowing water. I could fill a book, and maybe someday I shall, with my Vietnam war stories but here they would deviate from my tale of the Vesper 1964 Olympic eight.

While in Saigon I wrote letters home to my father's office secretary smart-alecky entitled, "Dear Taxpayer." She made copies and sent them to a list of friends and one such letter posted at the Cornell boathouse was seen by Charlie Butt, the coach of the Potomac Boat Club in Washington. To my happy surprise, I received a letter from him inquiring if I would be interested in joining Potomac for a crew to try out for the 1964 Olympic games a year away. I wrote him immediately in the affirmative and initiated the process to gain special military clearance, assignment in the Washington area and time off to try to become an Olympic athlete.

At that time qualified athletes in the armed services were being relieved of their assignments and given permission to train for the Olympics on their own. I wasn't quite sure how this worked but I thought I'd give it a try.

Soon after I had a telephone call from someone in Bangkok, Thailand, who asked if I would be interested in joining the Detroit Boat Club for the exact same purpose. Heady stuff for a raw Ensign in Saigon. Best yet I received a letter from Jack Kelly with an invitation from the Vesper Boat Club which had a similar Olympic proposal.

I had memories of losing to Vesper the summer before so I figured that it must be the most worthy of those three clubs. Additionally, I was somewhat smitten with a lady living in my home area of New York's Westchester County. Philadelphia was closer to her than Washington or Detroit. So once again, I did the right thing for the wrong reason.

I left Saigon in February of 1964 and reported in to the Fourth Naval District Headquarters, luckily in Philadelphia, the first week in March. I had no idea of what was going to happen next. My Olympic aspirations were not yet very intense and I really did not know what I was doing. I stumbled and bumbled my way to No. 10 Boathouse Row and threw myself at the mercy of those in charge.

I told my Navy boss that my schedule would be something like this: Row from 8 a.m. until 10 a.m., then land strength training until noon, lunch and a bit of rest before hitting the water again from 2:30 until 4:30, followed by additional weight lifting and running. The good boss, Commander Wolfe, bought it and felt that I would be too busy to take on any Navy responsibilities. He asked that I come in semimonthly to pick up my pay check and let him know how I was doing. He later told me that it would be appreciated if, instead of shorts and a tee shirt, I wore long pants and perhaps a sport coat for those meetings.

My actual schedule at Vesper was more like on the water at 5:30 and row until 7:30, home for breakfast and on the first tee by 9. Lunch came after the 18 holes and then a nap before reporting back to the boathouse at 5 o'clock. We rowed until darkness overtook us and then it was home and to bed. My rowing and golf handicap improved greatly during those early months at Vesper.

14

Spring Rows

The Schuylkill in spring is a busy river. Because crews from the schools, colleges and clubs all have different schedules there is always room for one more shell on the three mile stretch of water north of the dam—just down the slope from Philadelphia's magnificent Art Museum. No pleasure craft use this stretch of water and it is near perfect for rowing.

While the city's spring weather is mild compared to what I knew at Cornell, I found it cold and blustery that March of 1964, far different from the languorous tropical climate I had left in Vietnam.

I had no guess of the Vesper intention Jack Kelly might have in mind for me. So I did only as I was told by coach Rosenberg and trainer Dietrich Rose. What came back to mind was the take a low profile advice from Kent's Tote Walker before I went to Cornell, and that proved perfect as I worked my way into Vesper's elite echelon. Follow directions without question. Do what you are told by the coaching staff. Do not compare styles. Do not question methodology. Be quiet. I had to add one more as I went along. Ignore the Amlong brothers, especially if they might try to tell me to do things their way.

We had two practices daily, beginning with a sunrise row and ending in the dark of early evening. Morning rows were generally in the small boats, pairs or fours, and we were on our own with little coaching. The afternoons were more formally structured, dividing time between small boats and the eight. In March, we often replaced the second workout with weightlifting at the Philadelphia Athletic Club on Broad Street, where Kelly owned a piece of the action.

Vesper's rowing style was different from the long low stroke that I had known. At Cornell we rowed with the oars long in the water, applying a lot of body layback at the finish of the stroke when our hands came quickly away from our bodies. This was followed quickly with the seat slide forward, slowly decelerating before the next stroke as our bodies compressed in preparation for the next catch of the oars. If there was a beginning of the stroke cycle at Cornell, it came with the oarsman reaching out fully ready to grab the next catch of his oar in water.

The Vesper stroke, new to me, required a little more sitting straight at the finish, and after the blade came out of the water the hands, shoulders, and the seat slide went forward in a slow progression at constant speed—ready to take the next stroke without any pause at the catch.

Cornell's style was designed to produce optimum performance at about a rate of 28 to 33 strokes per minute while the Vesper style aimed at rowing in the range of 36 to 39 strokes per minute.

Bear with me a moment longer. The Vesper stroke started at the finish, with the shoulders and body in a bow and you kind of rocked into the next stroke, gaining momentum as you came up the slide for the next catch, or entry into the water. This was different as well. We vigorously attacked the water with a hard bent-arm catch while at Cornell we had carefully placed the oar in the water before pulling away.

Approaches too were different, technically and psychologically. At Cornell we accepted implicitly what the coach instructed. At Vesper, as more experienced athletes, we were told not only what to do but we were expected to understand and embrace the theory behind it. This was a much more democratic system and it worked.

While the cycle of a racing stroke takes less than 1.6 seconds to execute, immeasurable hours, days and weeks—a lifetime of rowing—is spent perfecting that repeated motion.

Lacking the indoor rowing tanks found as standard features at most colleges, Vesper used a crude rowing seat and an outrigger affixed to the dock to train new athletes. Allen Rosenberg spent hours with me in that box where he could touch and bend my body to the proper angles explaining how and why he wanted me to modify my stroke. He had the ability to clarify difficult, technical concepts to me—to any athlete-explaining what he wanted in several different ways until finally the rower's brain might light up and all would make sense.

Unlike college programs, Vesper oarsmen spent a lot of time in the boats smaller than the eight-oared shell because there individual mistakes in technique are readily apparent. What became the Vesper eight was most often divided into various pairs: the Amlong brothers, the Yale duo, Hugh Foley and Stan Cwiklinski, Bill Knecht and myself. All of us were experienced in the fours and, in addition, we were encouraged to take out a single scull and row alone.

Vesper's expertise in such small boats gave us an advantage over most American competition since we all had a feel for what makes a boat move. This coaching technique requires considerable time, abundant boats, and is difficult to supervise since pairs and fours cannot easily be kept together for one coach to oversee.

Stan Pocock, of the Seattle family that has built racing shells for almost a century and author of a delightful memoir entitled "Way Enough," reflected upon the years he had spent coaching at the Lake Washington Rowing Club. He advised, "Superior eight-oared crews can only be developed from superior small-boat crews. With this in mind, have the men train in self-selected small boats. Bringing those up to Olympic caliber would be our first priority. Once—or better to say if—we have some small boats that move fast, we could try different combinations to see whether a good eight showed itself."

Pocock commented about the surprising Vesper 1964 triumph. "The Vesper Boat Club won the trials over our university crews (rowing in Pocock shells)…and I found some consolation in knowing that they trained largely in small boats…Vesper won with the same scheme that I had wanted to use at Lake Washington. So much for dreams."

We rowed six days a week in all kinds of weather, and we killed ourselves. When we were not rowing, we weightlifted—tortured our bodies by holding heavy weights (20 pounds) cradled in our arms, squatting and then jumping as high as we could in sets of 20. After five sets of these it was difficult to climb the steps to our apartments.

But train we did, together and without complaint, under the leadership of our club captain, Dietrich Rose. March trudged into April and by May there were hints of results, some good rows.

I regret that I did not keep a log of those times of slugging it out—keeping our heads above the waters. I never felt any pressure of competition—or politics—from within the club for seats in the Olympic trials boats. Looking back, I may have been naive about club rowing. I trusted categorically the judgment of the coach, the wisdom of the club's officers and the integrity of my fellow oarsmen. I was working only to improve myself in my situation—stroke for the eight, The Big Boat. I rowed without thinking of any goals beyond the practice at hand.

Socializing off the water was not part of the Vesper world. I was too tired to do much after workouts except go home, eat, perhaps walk the public golf course near my apartment just off Fairmont Park five miles north of Boathouse Row, sleep, and return to the boathouse for the next practice.

I did not take much interest in the other guys, nor did they in me. I avoided the Amlong brothers like the plague. Budd and Clark were a bit too close and Yale-chummy. Stan Cwiklinski and Hugh Foley, balancing school work and rowing, were a little too young to have interests similar to mine. Zimonyi worked full time and did not speak enough English to be sociable, and Bill Knecht juggled life as an oarsman, a father of five, and an executive with his own contracting business.

Each of us had an agenda and we tended to stay out of one another's way when not rowing. This was hardly the way it had been in prep school or college where your crew mates were also best friends. But we shared a collective intent—to be the best we possibly could be in all we attempted on the water. When we got those oars in our hands, we were coming all together.

15

The Rest of the Vesper Oarsmen

As we gained performance results rising to the huge Kelly-Rosenberg expectations, the Vesper boat house seemed to take on new life. We needed people to row against us, to test us. They appeared—indispensable yet nearly invisible.

The Flanigan brothers were still there, even though both had decided medical school was more important than perpetual rowing. Don Flanigan had a small regret. He told me that 15 years after giving up rowing to begin medical school, he discovered he had been in the top two per cent of those passing the entrance examination. "Had I known that, I would have taken another year off in order to make the team. I regretted missing the boat after you guys won, but I got over it quickly."

The twins continued because they liked so much to row and did well in their races, in spite of not sustaining the intensity of those working towards the Tokyo goal. The Flanigan brothers never complained that they were screwed or that they should have made the team. They were the exact opposite of the Amlong brothers in that they were perfect gentlemen. Perhaps they were not nasty enough to make the big eight anyway, in that it evolved into huge guys getting up huge hates against our closest competition. Still, the Flanigans were very much the making of Vesper in 1964.

Another quiet giant who did not aspire to Olympic heights was Joe Griepp, a former college oarsman from St. Joseph's who later coached there. Joe was teaching German at a prep school and his dedication lay foremost with his teenage pupils.

Two former Cornell oarsmen, arriving too late to be taken seriously, had been sent by the military to Vesper to try out. Bob Ratkowski of the Army and Al Thomason of the Navy, both lieutenants, gave the opportunity all they had although they never threatened to unseat someone from the big eight. Allen Rosenberg claims that Thomason "almost punched me out for not putting him in." It wouldn't have been much of a spectator event because the differences between the two were a foot in height and about 80 pounds.

Another Cornellian, Tony Taylor, appeared and joined Ratkowski in a pair-without-coxswain for the Olympic trials in August. But to no avail.

Walter Birbeck, another Philadelphian who had had participated in the Tokyo pre-Olympic regatta, won a seat in the Vesper B eight which fared poorly in the trials. To my recollection Thomason and Birbeck were the only ones deeply disappointed for not making the big boat. Birbeck quit rowing and never again appeared at the club. I do not remember him attending any of the intensive workouts in the early spring and maybe he was still with his college team. In any event there were several others in his situation who nevertheless continued to support the club effort.

Chet Riley, an Air Force lieutenant, arrived at the boat house late in April, too late to be a contender for the boat. Because Riley had been a talented oarsman at Massachusetts Institute of Technology, Kelly had written the Air Force on his behalf and he was released from pilot training six weeks early. That cost him the opportunity to become a fighter pilot. Kelly may have sustained his life in that Chet never had to fly any combat missions over Vietnam.

He did fly 3,700 hours in command of a military transport, the C-135 airplane, ferrying personnel to 35 countries but mostly to and from Vietnam. Riley recently finished his flying career as a senior pilot for American Airlines.

He had arrived at Vesper out of shape but worked hard in his attempt to catch up. He told me years later, "I wasn't screwed. I got there late and I simply could not beat out the established rowers. The best guys were in the boat and I could not catch up nor keep up. I have no bad feelings. It was the strongest eight I had ever seen, and the intensity of the focus was amazing. The selection of the eight was fair and I was pleased simply to be a part of the making of it."

Riley became a close friend during the summer training and when not golfing we sometimes rowed a pair together just for the fun of it. He was often assigned to row a pair with Don Horvat who came to America via Canada from the part of Yugoslavia that is now Croatia.

Don, who would get upset when we called him a Yugo, was a brilliant RCA engineer and eventually started his own successful company. He never looked like a good oarsman, and was not taken seriously, but he brightened everyone's day. He died too early but his son, who rowed at Princeton, is continuing the Horvat legacy at Vesper, recently serving as its president.

Vesper also had a stable of scullers who kept the boat house busy and alive. The club continued to win every point trophy in regattas in which most of the members rowed because we could win almost all races. These were good days yet the club was not known for its social ambiance. Friendships were made on the basis of performance on the water, not in the bar room. Vesper was a racing club about to prove that to the world.

16

The Popularity of Rowing

The Naval Academy's defeat in Rome had its positive side. The rising popularity of amateur rowing lifted the standards and doors opened to the clubs as the sport's rowing establishment galvanized to get the Olympic gold medals back for the premier eight-oared event. No longer was the sport in the sole possession of the colleges.

Rowing has often been a kind of religion to those addicted to its racing aspects. The competitive side was first made popular because its pioneer academic institutions were—still are—among the best the world has to offer. Other colleges wished to emulate the forerunners.

The oldest intercollegiate athletic contest in the U.S. is the Harvard-Yale crew race, held annually since 1852. The eight Ivy League colleges have supported rowing squads for generations. The top prep schools in New England offer rowing as a gentlemanly sport to help prepare the student for the rigors of higher education. The provenance probably was rowing in England where the annual Boat Race between Cambridge and Oxford and the Henley Royal Regatta are cultural commemoratives like Boxing Day.

Right or wrong, rowing has long been considered an elitist activity. It can also be said that the better the academic reputation of the institution, the better its rowing program. I like to believe that good rowing takes intense concentration, a deep desire to achieve, a fastidiousness for perfection, and an innate appreciation for the beauty of the motion and surroundings of the activity. These are elements that contribute to the rowing athlete being a good student in the first place, explaining why good oarsmen are drawn to good schools, or visa versa. It is a difficult concept for lay persons to comprehend.

The grandfather critic of rowing was Frank Howard, the onetime football coach and then athletic director at Clemson University in South Carolina which had no crew. Howard once said famously, "I will never support a sport where you sit on your ass and go backwards."

Susie Lueck, coach of the successful rowing program at Clemson has said, "I am sure that he (Howard) rolled over a few times in his grave after we added women's rowing as a varsity sport in 1998." She went on to brag. "We've been consistently ranked among the top 20 women's crews nationally at the Division I level and we have 70 student-athletes on our roster."

Rowing was given a huge boost by the Title IX legislation which mandated equal opportunity for women's athletics at academic institutions receiving federal funding. Thus the state colleges with expensive big-time basketball and football programs were required to provide more athletic opportunities for women students. Rowing affords the opportunity to have women participate—at a minimal cost—in numbers almost equal to that of the varsity football squads, thus satisfying one demand of the federal mandate.

Apart from the intercollegiate athletic scene, the prodigious interest in physical fitness among Americans aided the outreach of rowing. College graduates may continue in the sport in club programs and competitions at masters, veterans and senior levels. Their enthusiasm has been infectious for others who never rowed in school or college. It is common now to find people in their eighties or even nineties rowing for exercise and even racing on occasion. Membership in the United States Rowing Association has increased 20 fold since 1964, Vesper's victorious Olympic year. When I pass by a regatta site I cannot help but notice the supportive stickers on the windows and bumpers of the rowers' cars and vans which tell me how proud they are of their sport and how they want everyone to know it.

It is my observation too that rowing has what I call a participation benefit having nothing to do with winning a race, or a trophy. All those who compete are considered winners, a notion made so definitive in the wonderful Special Olympics where impaired athletes of every kind are cheered for their participation.

This concept can also be found in distance running events, like the big-city marathons held in all parts of America drawing thousands of participants. The Boston or New York marathons may have two single winners—one man, one woman—but all of the thousands that finish are never considered losers.

Rowing in the autumn months has adopted a concept from England called Head Races in which crews row independently over a set course racing against the clock. The best times distinguish the best crews and none are disgraced. These head races are found in many places but the precursor was Boston's Head of the Charles, now in its third decade and attracting crowds estimated as high as 90,000 on the final Sunday in October.

I like to believe that the Vesper achievement of 1964 acted as a jump-start for the growth and betterment of rowing.

17

Spring Training Ends With First Official Race

The Vesper Olympic aspirants logged countless miles on the Schuylkill River in the early spring months, but little can be recalled of any by our crew. Like childbirth for a mother I would suppose, the pain and the agony fades after the event.

As I have said we rowed twice a day, the morning session less formal and structured than the early evening row. The river belonged to Vesper in the morning, too cold and dreary—frost on the dock at sunrise—for recreational oarsmen. Evening rows were generally held after the schoolboy and college oarsmen had departed. We greeted the sun in the morning and we put it to bed in the evening. These painful miles were logged like money in the bank, security to call up later for challenges certain to arise. We built a foundation, each stroke like a stone in a pyramid. It was both wonderful and dreadful—only a masochist could really like preseason rowing but perhaps the best oarsmen are just that.

Finally, with the ice and snow behind us, the trees along the Fairmount Park riverbank burst quickly into green, the azalea gardens near the Art Museum ablaze with beautiful pastel colors. Spring moved as quickly as the progression of our crews.

From the time we left the dock to the time we returned we were in continual motion, either rowing full pressure or at the lightest paddle, just enough to keep the blood flowing. We had a brief menu of practices, including timed 500 meter pieces at racing cadence, pyramids of between 300 and 600 hard strokes and less frequently, long sustained rows. A typical 600 stroke pyramid included three ten stroke full pressure bursts at our racing cadence of about 37 strokes per minute, with the same number of slow-motion rest paddles between them, followed by three bursts of 20 strokes with equal rests, three of 30 with rests, six of 40. Then you would come down the ladder with three of 30, three of 20 and finally three of 10.

That would amount to an exhausting 600 pressure strokes with the same number of paddle strokes in between. The Germans call this method of training "farkenspiel" or "fahrtlichs", which translates to speedplay. It never fit well in the cocktail party circuit to say we rowed what we pronounced as "fartlicks" at Vesper but then we were rarely on the cocktail party circuit while in training.

We alternated this workout with a series of 500 meter sprints in which we rowed a mini-race distance against the clock, one fourth of the standard 2,000 meter course. Rest between these sprints was closely timed and we were allowed only double the actual time of the sprint—about three minutes—to recover before the next. These sprints were killers but they rapidly worked us into superior shape. Unlike our European counterparts we also took occasional long rows at a lower cadence, yet at full pressure. This helped us keep the swing and rhythm of the boat.

We never stopped to rest, never paused while the coach lectured on stroke technique, and never let our heartbeat settle too low once we were in the shell. Practices were shorter than those to which I had been accustomed, but each was twice as intense. Since we were not all buddies, we were often at each others throats. We got in the boat, did our work, got out of the boat and went home. The less opportunity to verbalize our anguish served us better.

The first 1964 race for the Vesper club was the New York Athletic Club's 98th annual Memorial Day Regatta on the Orchard Beach lagoon, soon to be the site of the Olympic trials, and we traveled to Pelham Bay where the Bronx meets Westchester County.

Relations between the New York Athletic Club and the Vesper Boat Club had always been testy and I was new to the politics of club rowing. In intercollegiate rowing the coaches appeared to respect one another and oarsmen assumed that fairness and good sportsmanship would prevail. This illusion was shattered at the New York Athletic Club.

Perhaps the contentions lay with the individual characters in charge. Jack Kelly, the consummate politician, was on the board of directors of the National Association of Amateur Oarsmen (N.A.A.O.) and was a major player in the American Amateur Athletic Union (A.A.U.) which he was later to head. The A.A.U. was the sports governing body of track and field, swimming and most other Olympic sports but not rowing, the responsibility of the N.A.A.O. When dealing with the New York A.C. Kelly came head to head with Jack Sulger, then president of the N.A.A.O. Both were sure they were correct in whatever stand they might take and those stands were rarely similar. Neither liked to admit defeat.

Jack Sulger had worked his way up from a beat policeman in New York City to become a lawyer and a teacher at the John Jay College of Criminal Justice. He may have rowed as a youth but I knew him only as the authority behind the N.Y.A.C. Sulger was a big man and always had a smile on his face. Based on his reputation, we suspected that his smile was brought about by the anticipation of screwing us. Sulger loved to create controversy. He craved the publicity that surrounded his actions as he believed that it created positive attention for rowing.

Sulger was instrumental in securing Orchard Beach for the Olympic trials and although on tidal water it was as fair as any 2000-meter rowing course in the United States. Sulger acquired funding from the 1964 World's Fair coffers to build a finish-line tower, buoy the course, and do some dredging. Orchard Beach was state of the art for the time.

As races go, the Memorial Day Regatta was fairly unimportant, insignificant enough that I do not remember its details. We made the trip to have an opportunity to row the course before the July trials to decide who would represent the United States in Tokyo. The starting platforms were not in place and we had amateurish floating starts. With six weeks to go until the trials, the finish-line tower was incomplete and the buoyed course a bit of a shambles.

The pair-with-coxswain, in which I presumed Boyce Budd and Emory Clark were to make their inaugural showing as club oarsmen, proved disappointing. They had a row-over, meaning they rowed the course alone as no one showed to take them on. In the pair-without-coxswain Vesper came in third and I do not recall if the Amlongs had a bad day or if it was a Philadelphia pair other than Joe and Tom.

But I do remember vividly rowing stroke in the four-with-coxswain, with Bill Knecht backing me up in the three seat. We were in lane one and were ahead by at least three lengths heading into the last 500 meters. To my surprise Knecht, considerably senior to me in both years and small-boat racing experience, panicked and called for a razzle-dazzle sprint. While continuing to maintain the pace I had set, I told him that I was stroking the boat and that he should just follow me and we would be fine. That is the choice of the stroke, after a quick assessment of the situation based on communication (either verbal of visual) with the coxswain and perhaps a glance at the competition. A coxswain can order whatever he or she desires, but only the stroke can effectively alter the cadence. It made no sense to take the stroke up at that time. I felt that in that moment I won both his respect and his confidence because he never doubted my ability and rowing capabilities again. We became a team of two, one to be reckoned with.

Following our victory in the four, we stepped into the eight for another 2,000 meter race. I do not remember our seat positions but we were ahead all the way until being disqualified 20 strokes from the finish for allegedly rowing out of our lane and interfering with another boat. We never made contact with another crew and to my knowledge we had not been out of our lane. We were disqualified by Brother Thomas O'Hare, coach of Iona College, and who is to question the integrity of a man of the cloth?

Sulger, the regatta chairman, would not override the questionable disqualification and ordered the race rowed over—without Vesper. A club all-star boat from the Schuylkill Navy was declared the winner over Potomac with Penn A.C. and the Union Boat Club from Boston trailing. Our Vesper time in the disqualified race had been a slow 6 minutes, 20.5 seconds.

The Vesper contingent, not a happy one, packed up and departed before causing further damage by protesting the decisions that went against us. I learned for myself it is best to be quiet and let others handle the political decisions. We were gaining experience, and sometimes a bad experience can be useful. I also learned to be leery of Mr. Sulger and the ethics of the New York Athletic Club, lessons that would prove meaningful in the days to come.

18

The Low Point Came in June

If there was a low point in the Vesper Olympic experience, it came the first couple of weeks in June. The college season was reaching its climax and we were just beginning our final push toward the Olympic trials. The boat was unsettled and somewhat slow. The Amlongs were calling everyone "pussies" and were determined to row in their pair where they felt they had the best chance of making the Olympic team. I was depressed about my failure to shine in the economics course I was taking at the University of Pennsylvania. Practices were dreary. All was not well at 10 Boathouse Row.

On June 6 we rowed in the traditional American Henley Regatta held on the Schuylkill. The race for the elite eights was won by the College Boat Club, composed largely of Joe Burk's former Pennsylvania varsity oarsmen but stroked by Lyman Perry, a Navy man, and included Dick Schwartz of Cornell. This crew coached by Burk led almost all the way and won by just under a length in 6 minutes, 28 seconds, slow for 2,000-meters but in a 15-knot headwind. Vesper was second followed by a crew from Syracuse and others from Detroit Boat Club, Potomac Boat Club and Buffalo's West Side Boat Club.

Our Vesper eight was stroked by the club captain, Dietrich Rose, and although I cannot remember the line-up specifically I know that I sat in the undistinguished four seat with Budd and Clark at 5 and 6. The best news of the day was that the big-headed Amlong brothers, who chose not to row in the "pussy" eight in favor of their pair-without-coxswain, lost to the Potomac Boat Club' s entry of Tony Johnson and Jim Edmonds. Their hats would fit them for awhile and we would not have to hear locker room banter about how great they were. It was an unsettling day for Olympic dreams.

I left the race course with a prep school buddy, Pete Baptiste, for a tavern on the Main Line where I made a fool of myself drinking Stingers. I should have been resolving to do better by working harder at rowing, or studying for a Monday exam at Penn knowing that a hangover on Sunday would not help the academic effort. Although I did not have an Olympic plan laid out the way the Yale pair did, this turn of events was not to my liking.

But if I was disappointed so was Jack Kelly who, in a deceitful last ditch effort to save Vesper, approached Joe Toland and offered him the opportunity to coach in place of Rosenberg.

According to Toland, "Kell gave me a call and wanted me to stop by the office. This was in June of 1964 and you guys were just getting together. I went to see him and he said he wanted me to be the head coach. And I told him not a chance.

"He replied 'Why not?'

"To which I replied, 'I would never work for you. No way. Out of the question.'

"So he got angry. He said, 'You may regret it. We have some good material.'

"I said, 'I have no regrets. I don't want to work for you. Get somebody else. I've seen too many guys come and go at Vesper. You won't fire me. You will never get the chance. I'm sticking with coaching at St.Joe's. And you can do what you want."

Toland looked back to a victory cocktail party at Bookbinder's restaurant after the Olympics when Kelly, using his nickname, said, "Hey, Spider. You should have taken the job. You would have been the Olympic champion coach."

Toland responded, "If I took the job we may not have won. Did you ever think of that?"

It seems that Kelly momentarily did not have any confidence in Rosenberg's coaching and he came close to making a major mistake. Toland greatly admired Rosenberg's technical ability to get the most out of a crew. Dealing with the eccentric characters involved might not have been a strength that Joe Toland possessed. Rosenberg certainly could be abrasive around our toughest guys. But they obeyed him.

We are fortunate that Toland had the wisdom, maturity and vision not to accept the Kelly challenge at this precarious time in the Vesper's fragile development process.

It was also fortunate he had kept quiet. No one knew of Kelly's heinous overture. Had we known, it could have damaged our established confidence in the great coaching of Al Rosenberg and possibly encouraged the brothers Amlong and the Yale duo to pursue their small-boat desires. The zeal would have fled from the eight.

The bright result of the American Henley weekend was the bringing together of the eight in final form.

Dietrich Rose had to exit because as a German citizen he could not row for the U.S. in the Olympics. To this day, Rose feels that he could have made the boat on his own merits and Kelly wanted him in the worst way. According to Dietrich, "Jack had an idea. He said, 'We marry you to this black woman I know and you will be eligible to row for the United States. I know the governor and it will work. And you won't have to pay anything when the games and the marriage are over.'

"I told him that I cannot marry a black woman, or any other woman for that matter, because my mother would kill me. I did not see the idea of being married to make the team but I would have loved to make the team the regular way. However there was no way to become a citizen within the given time frame."

You could say that Kelly was ruthless in his quest to bring the gold to Philadelphia.

So the stroke seat was open and there were no other candidates with more experience than I. The seat was mine for as long as I could hold it.

Rosenberg was next faced with the task of persuading the Amlong brothers to join his big eight. They had the physical strength but not the finesse nor mental mastery to row the pair consistently well—good work horses if only they could be harnessed.

What happened next comes from Sean Shea, the keen Vesper observer. He told me "I believe that in a great Machiavellian move, Allen plotted to get the Amlongs into the eight by setting up a match race between them and the Yale pair of Budd and Clark.

"I watched the race unfold from a car along East River Drive. Budd and Clark took an early lead but with 600 meters left the Amlongs started to move. With that Allen swung his coaching launch behind Budd and Clark and said something through his megaphone which may have spurred them on. They were first by a length.

"Of course at the finish line there was a huge verbal fight in which the Amlongs claimed foul since the coach helped the others during the race. But the genius in Rosenberg was coming out and he gained what he wanted, in that the deflated Amlongs realized the college 'pussies' were not so bad after all."

The stage was now set to assemble the pieces of the big eight for the final push toward the trials.

19

Push Toward The Trials

On Monday afternoon, following the American Henley, the same oarsmen assembled at the boat house possibly with a mix of attitudes but collectively at the mercy of their dissatisfied coach, Allen Rosenberg. The Olympic trials would begin in one month.

The formula for the trials called for two separate events, the first to select the eight-oared boat for the star event of the Olympic regatta. The second part would amount to selection for the other events, single and double sculls, pairs and fours. The advantage in favor of the oarsmen was that the contenders, who finished second or less the first time, could come out of their eights and compete again in other crews, other boats. It made sense for a sport that then had little depth in terms of international competition.

With their confidence-crushing loss as a pair at the American Henley Joe and Tom Amlong were now committed, or stuck, with the Vesper eight when we came to the dock that Monday morning. There were some conditions, as Emory Clark recorded in his journal. "The Amlongs rowed in the eight on their own terms, of course, with loud demands and advice always given, never solicited. They insisted on rowing in the five and six seats and Rosenberg acquiesced, even though it meant moving Boyce and me back to three and four.

"We didn't care as we knew, like everyone else, that we needed them, arrogance and all. From the day they got in the boat we began to improve rapidly, moving a length to two lengths faster each week, the difference due as much to their contribution, which was enormous, as to the departure of the men they replaced, primarily non-citizen Dietrich Rose. With Bill Stowe now firmly established in the stroke seat and Knecht at seven, there was no weak link. Stan Cwiklinski and Hugh Foley, the bow pair, had yet to mature but they had the basics, were tough, rowed hard, and didn't talk."

The new eight had two and a half weeks to prepare for the next test, the Schuylkill Navy Regatta of which this would be the 119th and to be rowed among crews of the river's half-dozen clubs on our home course.

We continued to row small boats in the mornings and then, in the eight each evening, a more intense coached effort of interval training. It was beginning to pay off. We never did time trials as such because the interval training method required maximum effort for small portions of the race and did not focus on pacing oneself for the full 2000-meter distance.

It hurts to give maximum effort for all of the six minutes that the 2000-meter course demands. The coaching concern about a time trial is that a rower may subconsciously hold back rather than give it his all since this is just an inconsequential test, not a race.

By doing the rowing in intervals—or in sections of the overall race distance that we call pieces—some rest is assured after about 40 strokes, or a minute and a half. The normal becomes the best, or perhaps, the best is the normal. The concept is that the rower can risk more in those 90 seconds, pull all the harder, with relief coming soon. Biscuit for the dog. Then do it over again and again.

When it comes to the reality of competition the race takes care of itself. Why? Because the adrenaline of the moment helps each athlete put together those interval pieces back to back for the full distance. It kicks in. Believe me.

Somewhere during the three-week training period before the Schuylkill Navy regatta we had a practice race against some other eight and Joe Burk, rowing's paragon as Penn's coach, followed in his launch, witnessing the new Vesper combination. At the end of the 2000-meter row Rosenberg called over to Burk and said, "My stop watch failed. I didn't get the time, Joe. Did you?"

Burk responded with a shy smile, not revealing the time which he may or may not have gotten, and said, "No. But your guys are very fast." Our time had been well under the six-minute barrier, which in 1964 stood as a standard similar to the accomplished four-minute mile in track and the ascendancy of Mt. Everest.

Vesper needed a good race and we got it June 27 with a sound victory in the Schuylkill Navy Regatta. My report here I took from the N.A.A.O.'s annual Rowing Guide and it is sufficient.

"Three new men in the boat gave Vesper Boat Club's big senior eight-oared crew just what it needed to romp away with the Olympic tune-up race and climactic final of the regatta on the Schuylkill Saturday. Vesper led almost all the way in the 2000-meter five-boat battle against a strong headwind to become the country's top contender among the clubs to vie with Harvard, Yale, California, and Washington two weeks hence in quest of the trip to Tokyo next September."

The commentary went on to say that the personnel "came exclusively from the armed forces when Lt. William Stowe, USN, went in at stroke to replace Dietrich Rose, ineligible for citizenship reasons to represent the United States, and the Amlong brothers, Lt. Joe, Air Force, and Lt. Tom, Army, went in at the five and six seats, respectively. Starting at a 40-strokes-per-minute beat, then slowing down to 36 much of the way before finishing at 38, Vesper won by two boat lengths in a headwind with the fast time of 6:10.9 over Joe Burk's College Boat Club."

That was the confidence building race that we desperately required and we all felt great about it. We also sensed that we had the talent to row faster and we set about concentrating on the eight, using the small boats only as a diversionary training tool. We were going for the eight's slot in the U.S. Olympic lineup and in so doing we were scaring away some potential club rivals.

At about this time the Amlongs decided to show their expertise as boat riggers. The Italian shell built by Donoratico, in which we trained and raced, had numerous potential mechanical adjustments which could improve performance. Or they would have exactly the opposite consequence if mishandled. Joe Amlong attributed his supposedly enormous knowledge of rigging to his rowing background in Europe. Tom and he assumed the roles of rigging experts on that background alone. Few of us wanted their assistance and for the most part their efforts were rebuked by the majority within the boat.

I remember arriving at the boat house one afternoon in June to find our eight sitting on slings in the aisle of the boat bay, mysteriously down from the precariously high boat rack where we had stowed it after our workout that morning. Because the boat was special, we stored it in the least accessible place in Vesper's crowded stowage area where clumsy novice rowers were less likely to damage it. Weighing almost three hundred pounds at 58 feet long, it took all eight of us, using great care, to move it. But the determined Amlong brothers alone had somehow taken it down and spent the whole day "frigging with the rigging."

The boat was too heavy to replace on the rack. Done was done. Whatever had been done now had to be undone and Dietrich Rose spent an hour on the dock doing restoration before our practice while the Amlongs fumed and groused about everyone's ingratitude. They were confident about the changes they made and, in their minds, they had produced the perfect racing shell.

Joe told me years later, "Tom and I lived rowing 24 hours a day, while the others in the crew went home. We could not help ourselves and wanted everything just right." They didn't appreciate that the rest of us were thinking rowing continuously too without having to physically change the mechanics of the shell.

The final tune-up for the trials was the Independence Day Regatta on the Schuylkill. We were flying high and won easily. Again I turn to the N.A.A.O.'s Rowing Guide report: "The Vesper Boat Club's senior eight-oared crew became club rowing's best bet for a place on the U. S. Olympic squad on the strength of a runaway victory at the climax of the annual Independence Day Regatta. Vesper's crew, stroked by Bill Stowe, swept away to a one-sided five-length triumph over Jim Barker's combined Schuylkill Navy eight after three rivals in the scheduled five-boat race had scratched their entries.

"Rowing at a pace of 44 strokes to the minute at the finish, after a 36 to 40 beat much of the way, coach Allen Rosenberg's boat glided across the finish line in the fast time of 5:58.1 for the 2000-meter Olympic distance. That promises good things in the Olympic trials at the New York A.C. Olympic course when singles and eights will fight their way to the Tokyo Olympics in October. Trials start Wednesday at Orchard Beach Lagoon."

After the race the boats were not replaced on the racks at our boat house but rather put on the trailer for the 100-mile tow to New York. At this point we might have had confidence that we would draw blood in the trials. But we couldn't put aside the fact that the last eight from a rowing club rather than a college to represent the U. S. at the Olympics had been sixty years ago—when Vesper won the rowing exhibition in 1904 at St. Louis. The college rowing fraternity felt it owned the Olympic eight event. Harvard crews had just missed getting to the games many times. California, Washington and Yale eights had all won gold medals more than once. We would be traveling to New York as unknown underdogs, a comfortable position to be in.

20

The Pace of the Race

Before we get into the thick of competitive rowing I need to point out various aspects of the pace of a boat race. Pace in rowing is determined by two factors, the number of strokes with the oar taken per minute and amount of effort the athlete puts into pulling through each stroke.

For the short distance of 2000 meters, the Olympic and FISA standard of about a mile and a quarter, pace in the eight is not as important as it is in smaller and slower boats like the pair or a single scull that are on the race course so much longer.

In other athletic contests, like a 10,000-meter race in track or a marathon, long-distance participants must learn how to conserve energy so they can last. Some have the ability to throw in a sprint, a "kick," and some don't.

Our interval training, which had recently been perfected for rowing by the Ratzeburg squad in West Germany, consisted of short "intervals" or "pieces" of the complete race at full power and at the racing cadence. Our intervals consisted mostly of 500 meter efforts with an occasional 1000-meter one. These were at full pressure, 37 or 38 strokes per minute.

The cadence of the race does not necessarily represent the power exerted. To get a boat moving effectively at its most efficient hull speed a higher cadence is first required and following the initial 25 to 35 strokes of the race, each crew should settle down to its most effective race cadence.

The Ratzeburg method had a preference of rowing at 39 to 40 strokes per minute while we liked a cadence of 36 to 38. Approaching the finish line in a close race, a stroke might choose to lead the crew in a sprint, taking the pace up as high as 48 strokes per minute although 44 or 45 is more of a normal sprint cadence. Usually a sprint is constituted as the last 20 strokes of a race but it might be the final 60 of a particularly close contest.

The stroke determines the cadence, with the help of a good seven man. The proper way to increase the stroke is to pull harder, getting the oar through the water faster, but keeping the same recovery time (if possible). To take the stroke lower, it is best to think of taking more time on the recovery without letting up on the power when the oar is in the water. Also, if you desire the stroke cadence lower, consider lengthening out the stroke—longer in the water using more lay-back or a longer reach at the catch. The coxswain, acting as the eyes of the boat, can inform the stroke if the opposition is "straining" at an unaccustomed higher stroke—or if they are loafing and hence saving themselves for the sprint. The coxswain can relay the intended changes in the cadence to the crew, but the stroke is responsible for the actual raising or lowering of the beat.

Mid-race extra effort bursts are defined as power tens or power twenties. These super strokes combine maximum effort with a speedier cadence raised by a stroke or two. These power strokes are taken to catch the opposition by surprise and to obtain a psychological advantage. If too many are taken, they become the norm and therefore ineffective.

Another danger of power tens is that a boat might subconsciously ease back following its surge. Also a power ten or twenty should be taken only after the rowers have gained their second wind. They are especially effective on home courses where the oarsmen can recognize land marks.

Harvard crews almost always gain on their opponents when they go under the only bridge, Boston to Cambridge, on the Crimson's Charles River course. If the bridge structure has separate archways, hiding one crew from the view of another for a few seconds, the result can be upsetting. The Harvard crews like to take a few super strokes going under the bridge and they often come out ahead on the other side.

I learned about pacing one time, after the Olympic adventure, while sculling on the Schuylkill. Although I enjoyed many hours in my single, I had not learned to pace which is so necessary in the single scull. It is an exacting craft because it seems to row so effortlessly while its slower speed, at least a minute over the 2000-meter distance, exacts the same toll as a very fast eight rowing the same course.

I recall taking a row with Don Spero, a wonderful Cornell grad who won the Diamond Sculls at Henley in 1965 and a world championship the next year. That day I had a special resolve to beat him, even if it meant nothing.

So we were rowing 500 meter pieces and I could take a one length lead on him in the first 20 strokes. He would pull even in the second 20 and then he would end up beating me by over a length. This happened on each of the first three or four 500's we did together. For the last one, I decided to hold back in the first twenty strokes, put more pressure on in the second 20 and pour out all I had left in the last 20. The result was I won by over a length, or about what he had been beating me when I was not pacing myself. That was when I learned about pace—something not necessary in an eight but critical in the single.

Too many power strokes can hurt a crew. In the early 1970's Ted Nash as coach brought a good University of Pennsylvania crew to the I.R.A. regatta at Syracuse, a contender for the national championship. Ever the inventor, Nash was seen putting ribbons around selected trees along the shoreline of the race course on Lake Onondaga. That night, at the regular coaches get-together at Raffiels Tavern, Ted's activity was discussed. Nash did not hang out with the beer drinking coaches who supposed that those ribbons marked the places where he wanted the Penn crew to take its power-ten strokes. After much discussion the coaches decided that it would be unethical to take his ribbons down.

However an enterprising young student manager from Rutgers was appointed to put ribbons on all the trees along the shoreline. The following day the Penn crew sprinted from one power-ten into another rather than rowing their best at a settled pace. They seemed to be killing themselves and confounding their coach while the opposing coaches smirked.

21

Finally The Olympic Trials

On Monday evening, July 6, the unheralded Vesper crew arrived at the New York Athletic Club's Pelham Bay boat house on its magnificent country establishment overlooking Long Island Sound. Our transport was a motley assortment of cars and trucks contrasting to the college crews with smart vans and buses.

Not wanting to stray too far from his sheet-metal contracting business while we prepared our boat for practice, Bill Knecht sat in his white Chrysler convertible talking on the car phone to his office. The college boys had professional riggers to prepare their boats while we did that work ourselves, with club captain Dietrich Rose supervising.

Many of the college oarsmen were grouped in orderly fashion except the crew from California busy playing organized frisbee in the parking lot. Our mature crew thought that a waste of time. Bob Whitney, Harvard's seven man, said Cal was doing it "to appear cool".

Joe and Tom Amlong set about looking over the college boys, offering them advice and generally making them feel uncomfortable. Chewing tobacco and producing the accompanying streak of spit, they wandered about causing confusion and discontent. While the Amlongs' teammates could hardly be proud of them we certainly were united in happiness that they were not on an opposing crew.

Boyce Budd recalled the initial outing at the trials. He said, "We were the last ones to go out for a practice. As usual we were dressed in rags, our normal outfits. Nothing matched and there was no hint that we were from Vesper. We didn't have practice uniforms like the colleges. Emory had on a Marine Corps shirt. Hugh was wearing something he'd gotten in trade from the previous year's trip to Japan, and with his thick glasses he looked like a leftover loser from World War II. We were all fussing around and shouting while getting our Italian-built shell ready for the water.

"Our coxswain was having a hard time controlling the group but we finally got in the boat and when we were told by him to push off some were still tying shoes, others were fumbling with the rigging. As we left the dock only three men were rowing and everyone was talking. Then a couple more joined in the rowing as we limped away from the dock and finally we all were rowing but one handed and apparently very disorganized. The college trained oarsmen on the shore were flabbergasted at this mess called the Vesper Boat Club, but we were loving it, throwing them off. It was a fun psyche job."

To this day I don't know why Jack Kelly insisted that we take John Quinn to New York to be our coxswain for the trials. We had been doing fine with Robby Zimonyi. According to Rosenberg, Kelly did not have a great deal of respect for coxswains and what they could do for a boat. To Kelly, who had primarily been a sculler, coxswains were a burden of excess weight that had to be carried along.

John Quinn was an innocuous little guy who, while he was small and of the right weight, appeared to be more round than tall. But he could speak English and perhaps Kelly thought that it was his turn to steer the big eight. Besides Zimonyi had a job and we guessed he could not miss work. In any event Quinny finally got the boat going together and we were out on the newly buoyed Orchard Beach course.

In 1964 there were no rowing courses in the United States that had lines of buoys delineating the lanes and this system was new to poor John Quinn. While the lanes were wide enough to accommodate a racing shell easily, each buoy was made of an 18-inch square piece of Styrofoam with a dowel the size of a broomstick through the middle and was anchored. Hitting such a marker could break an oar or cause a boat-stopping crab, although they were not a hazard if the coxswain could steer precisely down the middle of their line. There was about five feet clearance on either side.

Did I write crab? That is the rowing term for the dreaded glitch that can upset a crew's rhythm and even cause it to lose a race. Someone's oar catches in the water clumsily during the stroke and rather than a clean withdrawal the oar can dive down at the blade leaving the inboard end soaring upward. A bad crab has been known to lift an oarsman, caught by the rising handle end, right out of the boat, because the boat and men amount to about 2,000 pounds of momentum. It can take awhile for an eight to recover from a crab, to get everyone rowing all together again.

Our designated coxswain could not keep the shell in the middle of the lane and we hit the buoys on one side and then the other as we zigzagged down the straightaway. Before all our wooden oars were destroyed in this first practice we collectively stopped rowing, shouted, "OUT, OUT, OUT," and returned to the dock. Poor John Quinn was out of the coxing job. A telephone call to Philadelphia produced the wonderful Robert Zimonyi who was sitting in the coxswain seat the very next morning. Because of a wealth of experience on European buoyed courses, Robby had no problem with the markers.

Thirty-seven years later I had the nerve to ask Quinn what the problem was with his steering and he told me, "I later found that I have a sight problem called vision parallax which caused my inability to steer in the lane. Missing the chance to go to the Olympics haunted me for years as one of the three great tragedies in my life, those being loss of a child, losing that opportunity, and being fired from a job—in that order."

He became a fully licensed regatta judge and official and he told me that he had closure on the 1964 incident when he was selected to be a rowing referee at the 1980 Olympic games in California. The lesson I learned, and applied to teaching coxswains in later years, is that you should only steer by reference off of one side of the lane-marking buoys and not try to stay in the middle of two lines.

The arrival of Zimonyi did not mark the end of our difficulties. During a practice start the following morning, when the equipment was fully stressed, we broke a rigger bolt. We had to find a metric stainless bolt to replace the damaged one in a two-year-old Donoratico shell from Italy. While the college boys rested in hotel rooms Boyce Budd and I drove around Westchester County visiting foreign car dealers seeking the proper metric piece.

Back at the regatta site Allen Rosenberg had been informed by our nemesis, Jack Sulger, that our entry in the trials had been disallowed because it was received too late. This obstruction to our entering the regatta was not taken lightly by Rosenberg, an attorney, and he proceeded to secure a court injunction halting the entire event.

I separated myself from this distracting procedure, and refused even to listen to talk of it, allowing the boat house politicians to work it out. Kelly got in the act and after much discussion and debate, the entry was allowed. My psyche was not marred by this turn of events as I was able to tune it all out.

Our budget was tight and with the aid of my parents, I helped to secure motel rooms in Westchester County. We did not want to go into the city and so we stayed at the Tuckahoe Motor Inn near my Bronxville home. Several carefully selected teammates stayed at our family home. (I was not prepared to subject my parents to the Amlong brothers.)

We ate at a good restaurant in Bronxville called The Tap and were served ample food along with several pitchers of beer at each meal. It was a perfect situation and we stayed away from anything related to the regatta. I doubt that any of our Olympic trials competition handled pre-race stress in a similar manner.

Concerning the absence among us of any traditional approach to racing, Boyce Budd has said, "There seemed to be a pent up violence in the Vesper Boat—an irreverence toward all the 'nice' things about rowing—all the nice guys, the blue blazers and all that shit. We threw all that out the window.

"Let's get the best eight maniacs and throw them in a boat. I liked that. It seemed to me that there was a savagery about it that I really loved. I'd never been in an eight-oared boat like that. I'd been in Cambridge University boats where three of the rowers' names had the title 'Honorable' before Lord Somebody and two others who were brothers of royalty. Nice guys, tough guys.

"I don't mean to make fun of them but there was this pent-up anger in the Vesper boat that we did not have in England. All of us had something to prove. I did, Rosenberg did, the Amlongs, everyone. Rosenberg had a chip on his shoulder as big as a house. And everyone in our eight had the confidence that we were not going to settle for losing to a college crew."

There were 16 eights entered in the Wednesday heats. It was easy for a seeding committee to differentiate among the college boats because they had recently come through a full racing season. But the club boats were just forming and little . was known about them.

The favorite was the undefeated eight from Harvard coached by Harry Parker, who had once been a Vesper oarsman. The University of California's crew from Berkeley was unbeaten as well and Yale had shown some strength at the Eastern Sprints regatta. The old timers were speculating about which of these colleges would dominate and the Harvard alumni were so sure of the Crimson's chances that they had made preliminary plans to charter an airplane to take them to Tokyo.

Harry Parker later had this to say about the trials, "I think it's no surprise the press indicated that it would probably be a college boat that won. The focus was on the college crews. A club crew had not won the trials since 1908 or something like that. And we did not know enough about Vesper to know how fast they were, since they hadn't raced any of us.

"Therefore the Harvard focus was on California. Looking back that wasn't any surprise. In the Vesper boat all the people were very good and very strong but none of them had world champion credentials. Budd rowed on the junior varsity at Yale. I'm sure he rowed at Cambridge, but what's Cambridge? Clark had been in some slow Yale boats. We knew the Amlongs were good in pairs. All the credentials were good, but not overwhelming. Nobody knew how strong the combination was going to be. So quite frankly we were surprised how fast you guys were."

Parker had been tipped off by his college coach at Penn, Joe Burk, that we were doing 500 meter pieces on the Schuylkill, averaging a very quick one minute and 21 seconds. Burk had told Parker that he had better keep an eye on Vesper but there was little Harry could do. His oarsmen would not have believed him so he did not tell them.

He said, "I thought we had at least a 50-50 chance of winning the trials and Cal was the competition I was shooting at. We made up our minds that we were going to race as hard as we could against Cal. Vesper was the unwelcome guest."

The initial heat for Vesper was so forgettable that I had to look up the results. They had slipped from the minds of all of us. The course, mostly in a protected lagoon, had been dredged wide enough to handle six lanes but it was determined that four abreast would provide the fairest competition. In the opening heat we defeated the Laconia Rowing Association entry from New Hampshire by three lengths with Princeton and the New York A. C. trailing. The Laconia group was made up of college oarsmen, an all-star cast for the trials, and they had entered three eights.

Our time was the slowest of the winners of the four heats indicating we were not pushed. That first-place finish entitled us and the three other winners to a day off while all the losers raced each other in the repechage, or second-chance, heats to determine who would qualify for the remaining four slots in Friday's semi-finals. This day off also gave the Amlong brothers more time to skulk around intimidating the competition.

In the semi-finals the first two boats in each of two heats would qualify for the finale. We drew Harvard, the University of Washington's junior varsity and the Laconia boat we had already beaten easily. So it appeared that our race would be between Harvard and Vesper with both advancing to the finals.

Before our race the tensions of the Harvard-Yale rivalry were apparent. Budd and Clark appeared to be in a trance of anger and hatred. They had lost to Harvard while at Yale and revenge was in their hearts. Harry Parker, the Penn alumnus only in his second year as the varsity coach, said, "I think they carried a revenge chip pretty high on their shoulders. But I was a little bit new to the Harvard-Yale stuff then. It was obvious they were never going to forget they were from Yale and I was from Harvard."

In the semi-finals we defeated Harvard by two lengths in a time that was six seconds better than that of the other heat, won by California. Clark wrote, "It was a shell-shocked group of proper young Harvard gentlemen that found itself two lengths behind at the finish line of what was for us a most satisfying and not particularly tough race. Leaving the Har-Vards to the shattered remnants of their invincibility, we went back to our motel with the certain knowledge that it was ours—a berth on the U.S. Olympic team if some one of the hundred possible rowing accidents didn't happen to us."

Clark continued, "In the interminable 24 hours before the Saturday final, while our minds pondered each of those accident possibilities in turn, the outside world discovered us. Reporters called wanting to know who Rosenberg was, what Vesper was. I remember talking for half an hour to some guy from the New York Herald Tribune, who had obviously put his journalistic money on Harvard and had a lot of ground to make up.

"In addition families and friends started to show up. Joe Amlong's voluptuous sister-in-law spent much of the afternoon perched on my bed, which was nice, but not exactly what I needed at that moment. As is always the case, at the time during any athletic event when the athlete most needs to be free of outside distraction—to be able to concentrate, to block all irrelevancies from his mind—he is least able to do so.

"Perhaps it was the distractions, our relative inexperience, traipsing around at midnight the night before to find the Amlongs into their quarts of beer without which neither could go to sleep. Or the fact that we had been together as a boat less than six weeks. In any case we got off to a poor start in the four-boat final."

Because I was staying at home in Bronxville I missed the late-night distraction but I do recall a kind of tormented sleep as I dreamed of the final. Beating Harvard for me was not a big deal since at Cornell we had never lost to Harvard. I was more concerned about California's Golden Bears who in the three-mile I.R.A. race of 1961 had held on to a half-length lead over us for the full race course. They had over stroked us by two to four strokes per minute throughout the long race. I erroneously expected this Cal crew to die in a sprint. Even though our time in the semi-final had been six seconds better, I did expect them to be tough—the only obstacle between Vesper and Tokyo.

Our Vesper starts were never good and now we exhibited our worst. Because our Donoratico shell was so heavy it took some muscle to get the shell up and going. Our plan was to row our own race to the halfway point and then to take several power-tens to pull ahead and discourage the college kids. The rowing conditions were perfect with placid water and a slight tailwind. Yale was in the lane to our left, and Harvard and Cal were on our right.

After we took our normal start at 45 strokes per minute for 20 strokes and settled into a 37 cadence, we were behind by half a boat length to Harvard and about even with Cal. Budd remembers that Clark had a partial crab in this scramble to get away fast but the race was on and we could not go back and try again.

We churned down the course holding our own with Harvard and Cal as Yale dropped back.

Before the 1000-meter mark we could hear that Harvard was taking a power ten. After inching back from our poor start we were even and we knuckled down at Zimonyi's urging. Harvard's big move had failed to materialize. We made our move right after their failed attempt and were able to gain a seat with each stroke.

With 800 meters to go we took control of the race. Now it was simply a matter of not making any mistakes or allowing them to be successful in any attempted push. I looked to the Cal boat anticipating something special but they offered no surprises. We had no reason to attempt a fancy sprint and perhaps we did not have one, so we simply held onto the length lead and rowed for home.

The Vesper Eight leading Harvard and California with about 800 meters left in the Olympic Trials final at Orchard Beach Lagoon.

It is a joyful presence to have a lead and know that victory is imminent. We enjoyed the rowing. It was torture for Harvard though and they did not give up. They gave their all but it simply was not enough. We crossed the line with a little open water—a boat length plus or about 65 feet—over Harvard in six minutes and one second. Vesper had done the impossible and we were on our way to Tokyo.

Approaching the finish line of the Olympic trials, with Vesper leading Harvard. California on the right was third, with Yale taking fourth.

22

The Laurels of Winning

At Vesper, whenever we finished a hard piece of rowing, we never came to a halt or even a pause. We paddled away from a finish line with no power exerted, the same way a runner at the end of a race jogs for a bit before stopping. This was not the traditional rowing way of doing things. Some interpreted that routine as rubbing in a hurtful loss, as though to show we still had more in us. In any event, while the defeated Harvards were collapsing in their shell at the end, we paddled away from the finish line. Reaching the end of the lagoon, we turned about and headed for the victory dock.

We were surprisingly mature about our victory and the promise of things to come. No hollering or carrying on for the Vespers. I had to hold back my jubilation, nonetheless, and was near bursting with excitement as we pulled into the dock reserved solely for the first place boat. It was early afternoon of a beautiful summer's day.

The float had sunk to water level so loaded was it with Vesper friends and regatta officials wanting to congratulate us on our upset victory. Jack Kelly was beaming as was a pleased Al Rosenberg. Many of the spectators, making up a crowd estimated at 5,000, hung around to see up close who was in this mystery boat. We arose from the shell and, as rowing tradition mandates, proceeded to throw Bob Zimonyi in the water.

*Coxswain Bob Zimonyi being tossed into the Orchard Beach Lagoon follow-
ing the Vesper victory, with Hugh Foley having been pushed.*

A bank of photographers snapped pictures and asked us to toss him in again
which we did. As reported in Sports Illustrated, "On the third immersion Tom
Amlong called for an abrupt halt to the game. 'You guys better get it this time,'
he told the newsmen. 'He's got rheumatism, you know.' After all, you can't treat
an old man like he was just a boy."

*After the press photographers demanded a re-throw of Zimonyi, Boyce Budd
is included in the dunking.*

We returned to the shell for the two-mile paddle back to the New York A.C. boathouse. Rowing with one hand and waving to friends with the other, we may have confounded the crowds with our casualness. That, too, was a rub as conventional rites frowned on showing off. But we did little that was conventional.

After a victory, the row back to the boathouse is always a joyous one.

When we were out of sight of spectators and photographers on the paddle home we whooped it up a bit and let our sham maturity ease. It was a fun paddle but upon arriving back at the dock we restored the mantle of false modesty. Confronted by press and well wishers, we chose our words carefully because we knew we would be quoted. The Amlong brothers, who'd had poor experiences with media people, were surprisingly quiet and refined. Yet it was difficult not to wear a silly grin.

The national press gave a lot of coverage to rowing and the results of the Olympic trials made for headlines in many sports sections of the newspapers. Sports Illustrated's lead story in its July 20 magazine had the headline, "Anything That Boys Can Do...Men Can Do Better." The New York Herald Tribune led with, "Vesper Crew In Olympics, Harvard 2nd in Final." The New York Times had sent two reporters to cover the event and one, William N. Wallace, wrote a long piece with the headline,"Vesper Club's 'Old Men' Expect To Be Faster in Tokyo Races."

Both the California and Yale crews went out of their way to congratulate us and wish us well at the Olympics. Both surrendered their shirts to us—yet another college crew tradition—and they were most gracious. Good sportsmanship mandates no excuses for losing a race, and we heard none. Years later the Yale stroke, Peter Conze, told me they had suffered a crab at the start and never could get back in the swing. He admitted that they would hardly have won but had this not occurred they would have been in the chase rather than settling for fourth. He would never name the teammate who suffered the crab in a further show of the manner in which gentlemen handle this team sport.

Similarly the California oarsmen made no excuses. Not so long ago I learned from Tom Dunlap, a Kent School classmate of mine who then served as the Cal freshman coach, that the Cal Varsity felt they were grievously harmed at the start by the wake of an errant motor launch. Tony Schilling, who sat in the seven seat, still bears a huge grudge against the officials, I'm told. The referee, if he believed one boat to have been unfairly hindered, could have called off the race and had it started over again. This complaint, by the way, was never aired publicly by California due to the code of rowing's gentlemen.

We never saw the Harvard boys which seemed like a display of rather poor sportsmanship. It took me 37 years before I confronted Harry Parker about this and I guessed that he might have instructed them to ignore us. Parker said, "I didn't know the Harvard guys didn't come over and wish you well. It was probably more because it reflected the depth of the disappointment than anything else.

Also they raced very hard. They put out everything they possibly could. It was a deep disappointment so I am not surprised at that."

Parker's explanation was confirmed in an interview with Geoff Picard, the Harvard stroke who was immensely disappointed with the race—their best yet not good enough. Harry, at a young 28 years old, was most likely sharing the same disappointment as his youthful crew. One of the Harvard oarsmen suffered from a back muscle strain prior to the final, but this was not offered as an excuse for not winning.

Those Olympic trials of 1964 were a big deal with 144 of America's best rowers participating. I suspect many of those athletes are telling grandchildren about how they rowed there and, "Finished just behind the eventual Olympic champions." They're allowed.

The trials at the Orchard Beach lagoon go down as being one of the greatest experiences of my life. I cannot properly express what a thrill it was. I'd like to believe those at the trials who did not win had almost as great an experience and thrill by competing as we did. At least they had a fair chance of making the team, something today's Olympic aspirants miss.

Under U.S. Rowing's contemporary set up there is not a winner-take-all Olympic trials for the eight oared shell. Members of the boat are selected by coaches at national team training camps and so the joy of victory is denied these athletes.

We were all basking in our victory and had no reason to hurry in packing up the boat for its return to Philadelphia. I could only think about getting the USA uniform and being a part of the American team. Later when I got to my car in the parking lot, I looked around and saw that no one was watching. Only then did I let out the victory whoop, the one I had been holding back for hours, and dance a victory jig. I had no conception of what we would have to do and how hard we would have to train to best represent America in the Olympic games three months hence. I simply was savoring the moment.

Parents and friends were all anxious to share in our new glory. Poor Emory Clark spent this blissful time nervously dashing from one area of the New York Athletic Club's large complex of club houses and lawns to another because he had four different girl friends on hand to wish him well. None had been invited, none had knowledge of the others, and all wanted to share his time in the sun. By the end of the day he was a nervous wreck but somehow he pulled it off and each of these young ladies remained convinced she was No. 1. While the rest of us began to ponder the future, Emory was just attempting to live through the present.

23

The Coaching of Al Rosenberg

After rowing double workouts for months, the five days off after the trials seemed like an eternity. To the honed athlete it leads to restlessness and we were more than ready to be welcomed back to the Schuylkill after this layoff. My reflection is that this time off and the plan for the summer showed Al Rosenberg's coaching genius once again. He had control of our welfare and knew what he was doing—where he and we were going.

As an avid reader and student of athletes' physiological cycles, Rosenberg was aware of other sport disciplines in avoiding burnout or over training. In order to go faster, you first had to go slower. He knew how to push above the old plateau to find one higher than we'd previously achieved—with renewed vigor and hard work. This coach steered us clear of boredom with a careful mix of workouts emphasizing small boats complemented by occasional rows in the eight that would go to Tokyo. This was contradictory to what I would have thought we should be doing—after all, we were to be the United States Olympic Eight.

Rosenberg was out in front and alone, his curriculum misunderstood by the body of American sports coaches at this time. He was criticized by those without his savvy, I came to learn a few years later when I took up coaching. Back then I had no idea what was going on and, like the pawn on the chessboard, I moved as instructed without question or complaint. I don't think I responded out of irrevocable respect, mature understanding or deep set loyalty to my coach. Rather it was my ignorance that made me so oblivious.

Others were not so docile. Our four contestants in the pair-oared boats, the Amlongs and the Yale duo, now had more thoughts about their Olympic aspirations. Winning the trials in the eight had gotten in the way of rowing their pairs in Tokyo.

While the Amlongs now seemed satisfied by having made the U.S. Olympic team, Budd and Clark were not. They continued to believe that their best chance to win an Olympic medal, their holy grail, would be in the pair-with-coxswain event. But the eight in the sport's glamour event had earned precedence and they were stuck in the Vesper boat, the U.S.A. boat, like it or not.

Few of us knew then that both of these pairs had been promised by Jack Kelly that they could row in the national championship regatta the first weekend of August. The Amlongs and Budd-Clark had invested much time and effort in their small-boat training and they sought a dividend.

The brothers could give off a litany of excuses why they had never won a national championship in the pair, their aim for 14 years. They were determined to achieve the goal.

Budd and Clark had planned all along to row the pair-with-coxswain, a boat assumed to be for oarsmen large and strong but lacking finesse. These boats demand raw strength and courage and the Yale pair considered themselves perfectly fitted. Without much knowledge of the event—what it might require to win—they innocently took on an unsung paladin named Conn Findlay and whomever he might have along as partners. Findlay had owned the nationals for most of a decade and also owned two Olympic medals in pairs rowing, a gold from 1956 and a bronze from 1960.

As they had for their Harvard foes, Budd and Clark generated an inspirational dislike for a man they had never even met, Findlay, who had scores of admirers. They focused their weightlifting anguish, running exhaustion, rowing frustration and mental determination on the sweet, unsuspecting 6-foot 7 giant from San Francisco's big bay and the Stanford Crew Association. They had never rowed in a formal pairs-with-cox competition and had to be naive in supposing they could out row any Findlay crew.

Both these Vesper pairs trained with an intensity and passion that was healthy for all of us. The other four who had won the trials and were now established as the Olympic eight—myself, Stan Cwiklinski, Hugh Foley and Bill Knecht—had proven ourselves and were satisfied to rest on laurels for awhile. We worked out in the four with our coxswain, Bob Zimonyi; sparred with the pairs on occasion and conditioned ourselves with other wonderful rows. We were happy.

Vesper's entries for the national championship, to be held on that new course at Orchard Beach in the Bronx, were submitted on time lest we risk conflict again with Jack Sulger, the boss there. As is standard with most rowing clubs, Vesper entered a full card meaning most oarsmen were expected to compete in more than one event thereby improving the club's chances to compile the most total scoring points. The reward was the Barnes Regatta Point Trophy, emblematic of the best rowing club in the nation. Jack Kelly wanted that distinction for Vesper in 1964.

However our Olympic eight was made exempt. Rosenberg, almost forty years later, said, "Jack Sulger talked us out of rowing in our eight because he felt we were too good and we should allow someone else the opportunity to win that senior event."

The Amlong brothers were able to win their national championship medals in an uneventful pair-without-cox three second win over Potomac Boat Club's Tony Johnson and Jim Edmonds. Three seconds in pair racing is decisive and Amlong heads again swelled.

In the other pairs-with-coxswain event Budd and Clark were assigned John Quinn as their cox because Kelly felt responsible for his being put out of the Olympic eight and wanted to reward him for his dedication to the club. The coxswain in these shells lies down in the bow of the boat with full vision of the course and so Quinn had no trouble steering, avoiding buoys.

While I have the ability to forget the races that were lost Emory Clark has the desire and skill to record his winning efforts. In their planning for this finale in the pair-with-coxswain event Budd and Clark had resolved that if Conn Findlay was to be beaten it would have to be before the final 500 meters of the 2000-meter race because this gentle giant never let up from his initial devouring pace.

Clark has recorded the event as follows. "The Orchard Beach water was flat as a millpond and it took us awhile to get in our one hundred hard warm-up strokes, as it did Findlay. As both crews paddled back toward the start an official with a megaphone began yelling at us hurrying us to get on the starting line. The four other boats in the race had already backed into the starting platforms. But with the assurance of a two-time Olympian, Conn looked over and said to us casually, 'Don't worry, they won't go without us.' If I had been intimidated before, that innocuous little bit of cool was the coup de grace.

"At the command to go the nine months of training and determination reasserted. The adrenaline which had threatened to overwhelm me pumped merely at maximum levels. At the 500-meter mark we were a quarter of a length up and I suppose we were rowing at 34 strokes per minute. The cox of Conn's boat, Kent Mitchell, calmly gave them their 500-meter time and we both knew we were rowing fast.

"They were in lane six to our immediate starboard, thus we were able to keep good track of them—we being just far enough ahead that we could see them on our flank. The middle thousand was a matter of rowing along and watching them, a quarter to a third of a length behind, our fear mounting as we came up on the final 500, not able to shake them but not letting them get anything on us either.

"The 1500-meter mark came and went. We had only a deck length lead and our anxiety level approached panic. Without a word our stroke count began to creep up—to 36, 37 and 38. With 250 strokes left in the race their coxswain Kent Mitchell said, with a note of urgency, 'If you are going to get them you've got to do it now.' Kent's 'if' did it for us. They were human, Kent had just acknowledged the possibility.

"Then panic and our stroke went to 39, maybe 40. I forgot about them and worked on trying to finish each time, to be fiercer, more relentless on the pull through, to row each stroke harder than the last. To win."

Clark's concluded words: "Suddenly it was over. We were paddling, light...knowing we had beaten the legend. Our time was 7:19.8, a national record."

The race may have been over but there was a fight, a political fight, ahead.

24

The European Championships

Boyce Budd and Emory Clark, happily paddling back to the New York A.C. boat house, soon brought about contention because their victory affected Vesper's pre-Olympic plans.

In addition to the National Championship Regatta, Rosenberg had earlier felt that it would be in our favor to gain racing experience and exposure in Europe. He entered us in the European Championships, organized under the Federation International Society d'Aviron, or more easily said, FISA. I later came to name my wonderful Golden Retriever Fisa, pronounced fee-sa.

That championship regatta was scheduled for the Netherlands, on the Bosbaan rowing course in the Amsterdam Woods. Rosenberg accredits the idea of rowing in Amsterdam to Dietrich Rose, the former West German oarsman and our Vesper captain. Allen said, "It never would have occurred to me. I would have stayed back to train."

Kelly bought into the Netherlands idea and was able to persuade his buddy, Arthur Kauffman, chairman of something called the Philadelphia Olympic Committee, to come up with the funds to send the Vesper contingent overseas.

There were problems. Those rowing officials who had earlier agreed that the national championship winners of the pair-with-coxswain, Budd and Clark as it developed, would represent the U.S. in the Amsterdam regatta, were having second thoughts. In the pair-without-cox the Amlongs were the sole American boat committed to entering the Netherlands regatta. No issue.

Background: The good crews from European countries like West Germany, England and Italy expected the Amsterdam regatta to be a definition as to their investment—yes or no—in the long, expensive trips to Tokyo. Thus it would be their trials and an informal qualification for the Olympics.

Two hours before the flight was to depart for Europe, Jack Sulger held the airplane tickets in his pocket and the rowing bigwigs sat around in the pastel 1920's country-club setting of the powerful New York Athletic Club debating who should go. Who should get the tickets for planes departing very soon.

Conn Findlay and his partner, a Navy lieutenant named Ed Ferry, had made prior plans to race abroad and had even sent their shell ahead to the Netherlands. They claimed they should go to get additional racing experience for the Olympics.

And since no other money had been committed for expenses, and since the U.S. Olympic small-boat trials were a month more into the summer, the only Americans who wished to race abroad were Conn Findlay's pair.

But Budd-Clark had won the qualifying race and deserved the nomination, the airplane tickets. It had been decided four days before that the U.S. crews for these FISA European championships would be chosen upon their finish at the national championships. And the N.A.A.O. sanctioning committee approved of this arrangement.

However it was never thought anyone could defeat Conn Findlay's pair.

Within the faux Greek porticoes of the estate the New York Athletic Club faithful fondly called Travers Island, the debate went on. Jack Kelly, hardened from rowing political battles, fumed as he stood firm on the agreement set four days before.

It was quite a scene, the articulate Budd and Clark on one side of the assembled group and the mild Findlay and Ferry on the other. The rest of the Vesper contingent was packed and waiting impatiently to get the show on the road, and to get to Idlewild Airport and aboard our KLM Royal Dutch Airline jet to Amsterdam. Emory Clark, who years later remains bitter about the delay, said, "Those pompous asses, with but an hour to flight time and Kelly threatening dire reprisal, they reluctantly surrendered the tickets".

Finally we were safely aboard the plane en route to our first foreign competition as a group. We spent hours aloft sewing "USA" on blue sweatshirts that we had purchased at an Army-Navy discount store in Philadelphia. Because we were not fully sponsored we had to make our own uniforms. Coach Rosenberg forced us to drink a case of Hawaiian Punch that he had smuggled aboard the plane to counter the affects of dehydration induced jet lag.

It seemed to work, because after the flight we recovered quickly and drove to the course to familiarize ourselves with our borrowed race boats. We had brought our own 12'6" oars and heads turned as we walked through the airport. We had also brought along Dietrich Rose who proved to be invaluable. Dietrich understood how to rig the complex borrowed boats, where a fraction of an inch in the rigging could make a huge difference. Dietrich was also familiar with the political European rowing ways and could separate rumors from valuable racing tips.

We did not have a great deal of time to get the shells rigged correctly, but set about to prepare ourselves for the races three days hence. The four without coxswain presented us with problems, where in addition to rowing, the bowman must steer the shell with a foot stretcher attached to the rudder cable. Hugh Foley did a great job getting used to steering and the boat was acceptable. Surprisingly, Tom and Joe Amlong had no complaints with their borrowed boat.

Boyce Budd remembers his aggravation with the boat that they borrowed and remembers, "We had a real piece of junk as a boat. If we had our pair, we would have done much better, but we had a rowing wreck." Boyce and Emory had hoped to use the American Pocock shell that had been sent over by Conn Findlay for his own use. When Findlay learned that he would not be allowed to represent the United States in Holland, he ordered the shell sent home for his preparation for the upcoming Olympic trials. Findlay's new Pocock boat was recrated for return under the watchful eye of Budd and Clark, who thought it highly unfair that Findlay would not let them row his boat.

Rowing on the Holland's Bosbaan course was an eye-opener. A perfectly dredged 2000 meter course with buoys of the same system that had marked the 1960 Olympic Course at Italy's Castel Gandolfo. The Dutch even had internal circuit television screens to provide the 15,000 finish line spectators with a full picture of the entire course. The mammoth covered grandstand enclosed a huge restaurant. But best of all was the truck towed grandstand, where for about the equivalent of twenty five cents, fans could follow each race as it came down the course.

The 1965 Official NAAO Rowing Guide reported, "Fresh from the U.S. Championships only two days before, the Amlong brothers rowed to within 1/2 length of Germany in the opening heat, qualified for the finals in the repechage, but were caught in a furious final to finish fourth in the championships. Their time of 6:50 was overshadowed by the winners in 6:42.

"Budd and Clark in the pair with Quinn at the coxswain seat faltered in their opening heat, failing to adjust to a good boat and to make the finals despite a 7:22 effort for third place in the repechage. They clearly won the petites finale nonetheless and seemed to be better adapting to their environment daily.

"Much the same fate awaited the four without cox which seemed to row better at each outing. Rowing to within a length of the Dutch in the opening day in 6:35 (the Dutch had rowed a 6:11 on the same course two week prior) this crew rowed to 1 1/2 lengths of Italy (6:16) in the repechage. They also won the petites finales. Without exception these eight men from the Olympic eight evoked only favorable comment and praise from every European coach. There was concern that this crew (as an eight) would be in the same class as Russia and Germany."

The Amlongs were disappointed by their race and made excuses, although Joe admits that he had simply rowed himself out and could not produce enough strength to stay with Tom in the final. Boyce and Emory, coming off a huge high after beating Findlay, were clearly disappointed by their showing. In contrast, our four without was elated and believed that we had proved ourselves to our boatmates.

Our joy was short lived when we observed the eights that we would be racing in Tokyo. In perhaps the greatest boatrace I have ever witnessed, the German eight from Ratzeburg and the Soviet crew were never more than a second apart with the Soviets leading at the 500 meter mark by 4/10 of a second, by 2/10 of a second at the 1000, and by 9/10 of a second at the 1500 mark. Germany sprinted at the end to win in the blistering time of 5:50.65, only 2/100 of a second over the USSR. The Yugoslavian eight had hung close until the final five hundred meters, but faded to third, over eight seconds behind. Neither the Germans nor the Soviets ever rowed under 39 strokes per minute, and at the end, they sprinted at 44 and 43. The state of the art photo timer at the finish line recorded less than a 4 inch victory for the defending Olympic Champions from Germany.

We departed Holland seasoned rowers, unsure of how we might surpass the performance we had just witnessed. I was scared to death, terrified of an Olympic match up with these truly awesome eights. We had two months of hard work ahead of us, and that was nothing to look forward to with joy.

25

Training for Tokyo

When we returned from Amsterdam we were given a week off, Coach Rosenberg's wisdom working to avoid staleness and over training. He had us ignore the thought that we were idle at a time when so many crews were peaking for the Olympic trials in small boats in August. The Schuylkill was abuzz with zeal and intensity as those contestants honed their bladework, speed and stamina. When we again went on the river we concentrated on pure speed gains, a necessity and priority so obvious after seeing what we were likely to encounter in Japan.

We continued to row in the pairs and fours because that was where strength retention under full power originated. The eight was the only boat in which we had to shine. I think that the European championship exposure stood as an enormous awakening and a prod for us as a unit. We too recognized once more how good, even excellent, was the coaching of Allen Rosenberg and how critical the leadership of Dietrich Rose and Jack Kelly would be to our success.

Perhaps then, it would be plainest wisdom just to follow directions. This now was possible because the Amlongs were humbled a bit after their performance in Amsterdam and Allen had elevated himself in all our minds. We also had increasing confidence in Dietrich's ability to infiltrate the opposition to learn what they were doing and how fast they were doing it.

With his accretion of power as coach, Rosenberg at last changed the positioning in the eight. He moved Joe Amlong to the bow seat and Tom to the four seat, packing the muscle of the crew's "engine room" around Budd and Clark. Stan Cwlinski went to three from bow and the boat pulled more even with the stronger and more experienced Joe Amlong having the skill of "torque-leverage" that steadies the bow of the moving shell. The coach's disclosed reason for the changes fixed upon that one notion. However I quietly assumed that he was interested as well in separating the brothers so they could not easily converse with one another. The further toward the bow the Amlongs were placed the less I would have to hear them.

I was delighted with the new lineup as it was now more peaceful in the stroke seat. We continued our interval training, but never did more than six 500-meter pieces in a single practice, or more than two 1000-meter intervals, or more than 600 pyramid hard strokes. We had several long, uninterrupted, slower-cadence rows each week that reinforced the traditional American long-stroke "gait" and which made a difference in our final racing at Tokyo.

But we were not left to our own devices while happily training on the Schuylkill. Jack Sulger, who believed we were not training hard enough, sent word that we must race against both the U.S. Olympic fours headed for Tokyo too. He wanted us to continue to prove ourselves.

The trials in late August for the four-without-coxswain had been won by a Seattle group led by Ted Nash, a gold medal winner of the 1960 Games. In addition the four-with-coxswain trials had been taken by Harvard oarsmen out of the Crimson eight we had beaten in July.

Jack Sulger, in charge of the overall U.S. Olympic team, had a plan to break up the Vesper eight in two parts so we could race those fours, giving them some competition, and then have them combine to make an eight to race us the following day. This was scheduled for mid September. Although incensed that Sulger was tampering with his training schedule, Rosenberg had no choice but to comply with the wishes of the man who held our tickets to Tokyo.

In retrospect it was probably the right thing to do but we approached it as a negative. We went into these match races inspired by anger and easily won the time trial between the eights in a unmemorable row.

The previous evening Foley, Cwiklinski, Knecht, and myself, had raced the four-without-cox at dusk, illumination from automobile headlights along the East River Drive lighting our course. We were beaten convincingly by the Nash four but I don't remember putting much stock or heart in it. We had our own Olympic boat, the eight, and really had nothing else to prove.

On the other hand, the Vesper "engine room" four-with-coxswain rowed with a fair amount of Harvard hate and customary anger that only this combination of two Yalies and two mad brothers could muster against these nice young boys from the Charles River.

Emory Clark elegantly described what transpired. "With Robby steering, Tom Amlong at stroke, me at three, and Boyce and Joe in the bow, I was given two chances of beating Harvard in one summer. Although we had not rowed the four for some time we got out about a length in the first 30 strokes, took the rating down to 33 or 34, and gloated. We did not want to blow them away—yet. We wanted them to think that they could move on us—but never let them—to keep contact and watch them work, strain, sweat. I felt no remorse.

"Coming into the 500 at the head of the island, the finish about 65 strokes away, the suppressed energy among the four of us was building to an intolerable level. We were itching to go, to crank it up to 38 or 40 and open up five lengths on them. Boyce grunted behind me. Tom cursed Robby telling him to call for three strokes to build it.

"But Robby countered with, 'Vas de use, boys? Dey haf to go'. And he was right. They were the Olympic coxed four. They did have to go. It would only be destructive at this juncture to shatter their confidence, to wreck their self-esteem, to show that they were a poor second best in the U.S. Tom cursed some more but the adrenaline subsided and we rowed across the line still just a length ahead telling them it had been a tough race."

As a boat we were now gaining attention. We could hardly get through an afternoon practice without a flotilla of press, well wishers or the rowing curious following. We still had the solitude of the morning but the afternoons were exciting and heady for those of us who had never been in an athletic spotlight. We were invited to numerous send-off banquets, testimonials, and even to a Philadelphia Eagles football game at Franklin Field where we were introduced and passed hats in the stands to raise money for the Olympic team. The date of departure approached rapidly.

The Vesper Eight practicing on the Schuylkill River just prior to departure for Tokyo.

We were asked to participate in medical tests at the Valley Forge Heart Institute under the supervision of its head physician, Dr. Wolfe. The procedure included stress tests, oxygen uptake, blood and urine samples. The Amlong brothers were messing about and asking one another to lend some urine because they could not fill their bottles. The nurses, I felt, were hoping anyone but us would win the Olympics. Joe and Tom tipped the balance of ugliness when they presented the attractive young nurse with sample urine bottles so full by intent that she could not help but spill on herself. The tests were to be sent on to the medical archives in Switzerland for a study seeking to show that athletes outlive the average person. The tests, alas, did not examine the mental stability of the athlete which would have been of more interest in our case.

Ten days before our scheduled departure to Tokyo we packed our Donoratico shell, rightly named the "John B. Kelly" because his money had more or less paid for it. It would be in a freight flight to Japan.

Without our comfortable, fast boat for practice we found help from Joe Burk, the friendly Penn coach who invited us to use his American shell built by Pocock. Burk, a capital innovator, had designed and built a special outrigger that could measure the pressure that an oarsman applied to his oar at various parts of the stroke. A signal recording these pressures was relayed to a box in the coxswain's seat where five lights would shine when a rower pulled at maximum strength, compressing the gauge. In this way the coxswain could determine who was not putting forth full effort and the coach in his following launch could also see the results.

It was an interesting device and a fun diversion from tedious practices, especially as, unknown to us, Burk had rigged Tom Amlong's stress gauge at the four seat so that no matter how hard he pulled he could not light all the five red lights. "Tom, you are not pulling," commented Zimonyi from the coxswain seat whereupon Tom nearly tore the rigger off the gunwale. "Only four lights, Tom," said Zimonyi, as Tom got redder and redder in the face attempting to light all five lights. The boat stopped rowing and brother Joe walked along the gunwales to see what was wrong with the lights at Tom's four seat. There was much yelling and questioning from the Amlong brothers as the rest of us sat, smugly enjoying the scene.

I looked over at Joe Burk who smiled slyly at the unfolding chaos and I realized what he had done. It was wonderful, pay-back for all the aggravation the Amlong brothers had inflicted on Boathouse Row for a year. Zimonyi continued to ride Tom for not lighting up his lights and finally Tom yelled with his last breath "Shut up Robby. That fucking machine isn't working." It was a workout to be remembered forever.

Matters were going well as we approached the race of our lives. Then, with a week to go before departure and 500 meter times approaching those of the Ratzeburg eight, Boyce Budd was diagnosed with mononucleosis.

26

Limping Toward Tokyo

"Mononucleosis is a college kissing disease, for God's sake," I loudly protested. "What is an Olympic contender doing with mono?" I had no idea what it was but had friends that lost whole terms of school because of mono. The captain of Cornell crew, my roommate at the time, contracted the illness in his senior spring of rowing thus missing valuable practice time and races. I blamed his girlfriend (now his wife) for giving it to him. My Spartan social life insured me that I was immune from such a devastating athletic crippler. But here we were heading toward the pinnacle of athletic competition and one of our men had the stupidity to catch mono and ruin our chances.

Predictably the Amlong brothers figured Boyce to be a "pussy" for being sick. They of course would have toughed it out and their mono would have just vanished. The others did not know what to think and went on with business as usual. We put Bill Donovan, our lightweight spare, or Dietrich Rose in the boat in place of Budd to maintain a Philadelphia practice schedule and took a wait-and-see attitude.

Clark, Budd's sidekick, said, "I knew what he was going through and was outwardly sympathetic. In truth I was really angry at him. Mad as hell. How could he, after coming this far, threaten to jeopardize the whole boat, the entire effort, my Olympic dream? I hated him then. The wolf-pack syndrome—when wolves turn on the wounded and kill them—threatened to take over. But we needed Boyce desperately on any terms. He must have suffered the tortures of the damned. The others were even less sympathetic than I and the Amlongs ruthless."

Boyce had this to say, "Two weeks before we were to depart for the Los Angeles staging area en route to Tokyo it was hot and humid in Philly and I felt just so unbelievably weak, I couldn't believe what the hell was going on. So I went to a doctor and they did a blood test and that is when they determined that I had mononucleosis."

Rest and liquids were prescribed and the squad with Budd left for Los Angeles where, he recalled, "I was required to go to the hospital for more tests. My spleen was swollen and if the infection went into the liver, I was out of the Olympics. The problem was that in rowing you double over at the waist and if a vital organ like that is swollen, it can rupture. And if it ruptured, I would die. I would bleed to death.

"So it was pure and simple, cut and dry. If there was any enlargement of the liver at all, I was off the team. So every day I went to the clinic and they would measure me and poke around my stomach. Thank god the swelling stayed in the spleen. But they would not let me row. I missed all the rowing in Los Angeles. By then I had been out of the boat for something like three weeks. And of course I was dying a million deaths by not training. I did not even go to the workouts; it was an awful nightmare."

The rest of us worked hard at ignoring the fact we were less than 100 percent. We could not let Budd's problems worry us, because nothing could be done to alleviate the situation. Philadelphia had given us a royal send-off that included press coverage, dinners and meetings with politicians, and finally we headed for California feeling that we had the full backing of the city of brotherly love.

The reception in Los Angeles even exceeded the attention we had received in Philadelphia. We were housed in luxurious accommodations, had wonderful meals, were fitted for our Olympic uniforms, briefed on what was expected of us, and had the opportunity to row at the Long Beach facility, the 2000-meter course for the 1932 Olympic Games. Perhaps the best treat was a day at Disneyland as the official guests of Walt Disney. We sensed at last we were a genuine part of the United States Olympic team.

At Disneyland the entire team was given the run of the place, everything free including the rides. We were even expected to go to the head of the lines where we heard the comment, "I don't give a goddamn who they are. I've been waiting an hour." After the park closed, we were treated to a steak cookout, fireworks, entertainment by the inimitable Bob Hope, and a greeting from the mayor. We were given mementos, pictures, medals, and we got to wear the official U.S. Olympic parade uniforms that we had just been issued—a wonderful send off. Even the Amlongs were almost speechless.

In 1964 you could not buy official Olympic gear as you can today and so the uniforms were really special, limited issue and unique. We were given sweat gear, practice uniforms, towels, tee shirts and polo shirts, shoes, sneakers, racing uniforms, a raincoat, hats, and a suitcase to put it all in. The parade hat was a 10-gallon Stetson inspired by the fact that the Texan, Lyndon Johnson, was our president. It was like Christmas, payoff time for the American amateur athlete who received no compensation and was not allowed to accept anything that might be construed to be income as a reward for a best performance or a future endorsement.

Another highlight was marching into the Los Angeles Coliseum during half-time of the Rams football game, into the same stadium that had been the center of the 1932 Olympic games. How wonderful to have a huge crowd cheering our team, bolstering our dream.

We borrowed a Pocock shell for practice at Long Beach. It was so different from our Donoratico that we could not tell if we were rowing poorly because of the equipment or because Budd was not sitting in his six seat. Practices were shaky but we were able to work up a sweat and not lose too much of the edge achieved over the months of training. Because the course was an hour ride in a van from our hotel it was a pain to get there. But the practices made time fly.

I suppose that coach Rosenberg was getting nervous about Budd's absence because he began to substitute Geoff Picard into the boat in place of Bill Donovan. Picard had been the stroke of the Harvard eight in the Olympic trials and was liked by the Vesper bunch because he was not too "Harvard" stuffy. We did not feel so helpless when he rowed with us and we would use him in a pinch. We had several impressive 500-meter times in this borrowed boat and we felt it might not be too bad with this lineup.

Except our crafty Dietrich Rose thought something was odd because we should not have been rowing so fast. He spent hours with spare oarsman Chet Riley measuring the course's extra fast 500-meter final stretch and discovered it had been made 25 meters short since it was first laid out in 1932. Rose once more proved his worth to the Vesper effort.

Because Dietrich was not a U. S. citizen he could not be a member of the rowing team. Jack Kelly, who accompanied the team as an official of American Athletic Union, worked all angles to make Dietrich a part of the official effort. In an earlier appeal to the Vesper membership for contributions Kelly had written, "If it were not for the fact that Dietrich Rose is not yet an American citizen, he would have been on the squad going to the Tokyo Olympics. We had also hoped to have him included as assistant manager but this was not possible. We want Dietrich to go because we feel that he is essential to rig our boats and help Al Rosenberg with the coaching and training of the squad. His knowledge of international rowing is great and he provides a great inspirational force to the crew. For these reasons, I have made reservations for Dietrich to fly with the Olympic squad but it is necessary to raise some money to pay his fare." By hook or crook, Dietrich would not be left behind.

On September 27 in Long Beach, Rosenberg attempted to put Budd back in the boat, with or without the doctors' permission, to see if his seating could work. Without Boyce, Tom Amlong had been moved to six and Geoff Picard was rowing in the four seat. We set out to row some 500-meter timed pieces with the original crew that had earned the right go to the Olympics. Boyce was instructed to signal Al when he ran out of steam and could not row any more.

Emory Clark remembers, "We had done two or three 500's with more to go, when I noticed that Boyce started looking green around the gills. When he raised his huge right arm to wave at Al. I knew that it was absolutely the last thing that he wanted to do. One did not show weakness, ever, in that Vesper Boat. There was nothing I could do or say but that was never the case with Tom Amlong. Tom, who had moved grudgingly back to the four seat when Boyce returned, was wont to vent his finely tuned sensibilities at all inappropriate moments. So as the coaching launch veered in toward our port side, we heard quite distinctly a low guttural growl, 'fucking pussy.'

"For a moment, as the back of Boyce's neck reddened and his muscles bunched, I thought he was coming over the top of me. When I turned to look at Tom, he showed his shark smile which indicated how pleased he was to have caused the maximum amount of strife."

We were limping along toward Tokyo and we could not but wonder what our competition was doing, how they were faring. Were we the only ones having troubles?

27

What The Competition Was Doing

Although our coaching staff was assessing the strengths of our competition I did not pay much attention because I was too frightened after witnessing that race between the Russians, as I preferred to call them, and Ratzeburg in Amsterdam. I didn't wish to dwell on the competition.

However, 40 years later, I became interested in how and why we did beat the best in the world. This book gave me reason to research the competition, and I traveled to Europe and Canada looking up surviving members of the 1964 German, Russian, and Yugoslavian crews

The Russians were assumed by me to be from Moscow, soldiers in a disciplined army, huge unhappy men without spirit or life outside of rowing—stupid pawns in the Communist propaganda machine. I wanted to beat them for myself, for American democracy, and nothing I saw or experienced in Japan changed my opinions. With the later end of Communism and the breakup of the Soviet Union, I learned differently. Perhaps my impressions were wrong because they too were inspired by propaganda, American propaganda.

The "Russian" crew was not Russian at all. The oarsmen were from the wonderful town of Vilnius in Lithuania and they had no great love for the Russians. The U.S.S.R. had taken over their small country during and right after World War II. Rowing has a long history there, first introduced in 1885, and Lithuania claims to have accumulated 126 medals in Olympic, world, and European rowing Championships. Lithuania is active in FISA activities and is hoisting international regattas on the fine natural rowing course at Trakia.

The crew which had performed so well in the Netherlands in August was coached by the stroke named Ricardas Vaitkevichis or, as it appeared in the program, Richard Voitkevich. He died several years ago of diabetes and I have no idea about the proper spelling of his name what with all the little squiggly lines derived from the Cyrillic alphabet. I remember him as blond, less than six feet tall, and someone who never seemed very happy.

His crew had been selected to represent the U.S.S.R. after winning the Soviet championships, an event comparable to the United Kingdom's Commonwealth Games. The oarsmen were admittedly supported by the government after making the team but by no means professional athletes as we Americans assumed. In fact their club was small and the pool of potential oarsmen meager. Until they won the right to represent the U.S.S.R. their equipment was shoddy and rowing accommodations nowhere near the standards found in the United States.

I managed to visit Lithuania in 2000 and found the two of the surviving members of that eight, Antanas Bagdonavicius, who had rowed seven and Vytautas Briedis, the four seat.

They told me they had followed the interval training methods similar to those that Ratzeburg had perfected to dominate the 1960 Olympic games. They also did the intensive short-piece training methods that Dietrich Rose had brought to Vesper.

The rowing club in Vilnius is on the fast moving Neris River whose current makes it unsuitable for world class rowing. It was the place where youths learned to row and where most of the recreational rowing took place. The club's boat house was a shambles, shells stored outdoors with weather taking its toll on wood or fiberglass. I was astonished that such a club could ever have produced a succession of world class crews.

My new friends revealed several items of interest. In the last 500 meters of their close race in Amsterdam against the West Germans, they ran into a duck. The fowl was swimming on the peaceful Bosbaan course minding its own business before the collision. The duck made a big fracas with its wings and managed to tip a national eight off balance. The eight was leading by a quarter of a length at the time, and ended up losing by 2/100ths of a second. Such a distraction can cause a slow down and so the duck could have made the difference.

These oarsmen claimed their best race of the year came at Henley in July when they won the Grand Challenge Cup, defeating the Harvard entry there to help celebrate the 50th anniversary of the victory of the famous 1914 Crimson crew. The eight they beat was the Harvard junior varsity because the varsity was at Orchard Beach competing against Vesper in the Olympic trials. I also discovered that these same Lithuanian men had been in the eight that raced and beat my Cornell eight on Independence Day, 1962 in Philadelphia.

The Lithuanian crew had aimed at two peak conditioning plateaus and were successful in the first, the Soviet championships, but not the second, the Tokyo

Olympics. Antanas Bagdonavicius was not feeling well several days before the final at Tokyo, he told me. He had asked for a day off, was told the practice would be easy and go paddle. That he did, but the coach changed the practice plan. They rowed hard and he was pushed into a deeper malady from which he claimed he couldn't recover in time for the Olympic finale.

I learned that select crews trained on the Galves Lake in Trakai, an old resort town some 30 kilometers southwest of Vilnius. The Soviets honed at Trakai the magnificent crews they floated during the banner decades of the Soviet Union. A then new sports center included a gymnasium with a basketball court, a restaurant and bar (of course), guest housing for visiting athletes and substantial shell storage. Galves Lake is perfect for rowing because of few motorboats, smooth, clean water and solitude.

However the eight that rowed so beautifully in Amsterdam was not the same one that competed at Tokyo. As Vytautas Briedis emphatically said in my taped and translated interview with him, "Three Lithuanian members of that crew were found to be 'unsuitable for travel,' so they were replaced by Russians acceptable to the Communist regime. While not publicly stated, the KGB thought that these three might defect to the West. Their replacements were deemed not as risky. Family ties, professional status, political leanings and personality traits were the factors disqualifying these men and we could not question this decision. Our regional pride was damaged but the new Russians inserted in the boat were great oarsmen who did not slow us down. The fact that they did not speak the same language was a hindrance, but not an insurmountable one."

The Soviet crew traveled with a female doctor, Trajana Selivanova, who caused speculation among the American snoopers once we were all in Japan. Based on her seriousness, tough-looking demeanor and the black satchel she carried, we assumed that she was providing performance-enhancing drugs. At the Tokyo Olympics there was no testing for drugs.

A light moment for the Soviet crew with their Doctor, Trajuna Selivanova.

But almost forty years later Vytautas Briedis told me, "In 1964 we were too unsophisticated in the Soviet Union to know about drugging and she only dispensed advice, vitamins and the like. She had a good sense of humor and we all liked her." When I asked if she belonged to the KGB that was keeping track of the team, he replied, "Perhaps."

So I had been wrong in my assumption back then that the Soviets' demise in the Olympic finals was due to an ill timed drug application. My source was what I believed to be a credible rumor. These two former Lithuanian oarsmen, now free of the U.S.S.R., convinced me otherwise.

They said they had trained for the six weeks prior to the Olympics on the remote Pacific island of Sakhalin north of Japan. This foreign place had nothing to offer other than calm water for rowing. According to Vytautas Briedis, "We got very stale training in Sakhalin and it hurt our performance in Tokyo." A good idea gone wrong.

While we knew little of the Soviet rowers in 1964, thanks to Dietrich Rose we had a lot of information about the Germans we were to race. In 1964 there was only one German team, and it included the best from both East and West Germany. By 1968 the International Olympic Committee (IOC) recognized two separate Germanys. But in 1964, there was no secrecy. Because Karl Adam, Dietrich Rose's former coach at Ratzeburg, had shared his training methods with the rest of the world, we were using his interval training system to our advantage. Adam had once said, "It's the right of oarsmen to be trained by the best methods, regardless of nationality, race, religion or color." At no time did the German athletes regard our Dietrich Rose, who had taught us Adam's methods, as a traitor to their cause. Still it did make for a good story when Vesper turned out to be a challenger to the Ratzeburgers.

Of course this crafty Karl Adam was one step ahead of the competition, developing improved methods as soon as the world was copying his stale version of the previous year. He took his training methods from other disciplines and he particularly studied successful track and field coaches.

By 1964, Adam had been given carte blanche in directing the West German Ratzeburg eight. There had been no Olympic trials or challenges from other clubs and his eight had resumed a rigorous training schedule following its victory at Amsterdam. Adam believed improvement was a necessity for Ratzeburg to stay on top of the rowing world and he allowed his crew no time off. He hammered away at achieving faster 500-meter times, becoming obsessive, falling into the trap of more-is-better.

The key to the German team was their wonderful six man, Karl VonGroddeck. With great experience and strength, he was respected by all competitors. One of the valiant Ratzeburg members, Karl had been in the 1960 gold-medal eight at Rome. In 1964 he held down the six seat unchallenged. His first Olympic medal, a silver, had come in 1956 in the pair-with-coxswain when he placed second to Conn Findlay's boat. He was also an accomplished sculler who had won national titles in the singles event, accomplishments that Karl Adam admired over all others.

Yet Adam and VonGroddeck differed on the crew's rigorous training. VonGroddeck, the rock oarsman, said "You come with a suitcase full of energy in the springtime and you take it out bit by bit. But you must leave something for the race—not take everything out too early."

In reply Adam said, "There is no such thing as overtraining physically. Everything is mental. You cannot overtrain an athlete."

VonGroddeck recalled, "Karl Adam and I were good friends and I think he respected me as the senior athlete on his team. But things got tense and we had some disagreement about training. Adam was the 1935 German boxing champion and our argument got to the point where he wanted to hit me, which I could sense. So I went close and we were standing chest to chest so he couldn't hit me. I did not want to fight. I only wanted to ease off a bit on the rowing. It seemed like bullshit what we were doing. We were tired and it was beginning to show."

The Germans were having their problems and in spite of Dietrich Rose's contacts we Americans did not know of them.

The Yugoslavian crew was viewed as a threat but not quite championship material. The eight was coached by 24-year old Peter Klavora whose 22-year old brother Boris rowed in the boat. Both are now living in Canada, and have been active coaching and teaching. The 1964 Yugoslavian crew was somewhat smaller in stature than the other finalists in Tokyo, averaging six feet tall and 180 pounds. It was a well trained crew coming from Bled, the splendid resort village near the Austrian border in what is now Slovenia. Klavora was a student of the most modern methods of coaching and copied the West German pattern well. He had utilizing interval training methods on the water, and off water he had a good program of weightlifting.

They had rowed hard at Amsterdam, in close contention behind Russia and Germany until about the half way point. They simply could not keep up the blistering pace because their lesser size caught up with them. We termed their tactic fly-and-die which can work in club rowing but not against the best crews in the world.

At Amsterdam they faded to third place, eight seconds or almost two boat lengths back but a length and a half ahead of the fourth-place Italians. Had they not been caught in that dogfight between the Soviet and German crews, they could have been a closer contender.

Like West Germany, the Yugoslav crew was selected by the coach without trials or special testing. The eight was made up of four Slovenians from the Bled Rowing Club and four from the Navy Club of Croatia. Veko Skalak was the seven man in this eight and he had not begun rowing until he joined the Navy at 21 years of age, five years before. After six months of Navy training he was given the opportunity to do nothing but row which he grabbed. He became good enough to make the Olympic boat.

By contrast Boris Klavora started rowing while in high school because the Bled Boat Club was such a diverting place. According to Boris, "It was a bit of a whorehouse and a lot of fun. We learned to row while having a good time. We had no schoolboy rowing team. We started in a heavy training gig and worked our way up."

Two years before the Olympics the Yugoslavs developed a wicked weightlifting program, which included a practice of 500 squats with 85 kilos on the shoulders. They worked out in a small room in a basement where the boiler's heat was oppressive but obviously effective.

Peter Klavora, the coach, still suffered the effects of childhood polio. He lacked leg strength and struggled in the workouts that he had prescribed for his athletes. One leg was stronger than the other. According to Boris, "My brother Peter was stubborn and would not quit. He was more stubborn than he was good. We did have some friction between us, but when he gave up rowing and concentrated on coaching, it was much better."

After Amsterdam and their disappointment with a distant third they buckled down, concentrating on the eight with harder and harder workouts, perhaps falling into the same overtraining trap that hindered both the Russians and the Germans.

28

We Reach Japan

Having been dressed, fed and cheered we were ready for Japan. In terms of training Los Angeles had been troublesome—one hour in a van to go to and from a place to row in a cumbersome, borrowed boat. And Boyce still weak. Nervous sensations—whatever—in the pits of our stomachs intensified. There was relief upon boarding the Pan American Airlines 707 for the flight to Tokyo broken only by a fuel stop in Anchorage.

The big jet planes were only five years old or so in 1964 and though they went fast, our charter posed a problem for some of the finest athletes in the world. It was not suited for tall oarsmen or taller basketball players, many tense and uncomfortable.

Coach Rosenberg again had us bring those cans of fruit punch allegedly to avoid jet lag and dehydration. Following a meal the athletes struggled to find places to sleep, trying out the aisle and even going under the seats. Huge athletes were sprawled everywhere. Perhaps not a great idea, because in an emergency the stewardesses could not have moved about. The smart pilot wiggled his controls wobbling the plane and announced we were experiencing turbulence. Everyone take their seats and fasten seat belts.

There was lots of grumbling, moaning, and as soon as the passenger cabin was back in order the turbulence ceased. I'd had about 70 hours of civilian pilot's experience and was sitting with Chet Riley, an Air Force jet pilot. We quickly caught on to what the Pan Am pilot had decided was the way to restore order in his passenger cabin and we relished that—about the only light moment in the interminable flight.

Emory Clark, still mad at Budd over the mono exposure, sat apart from us and next to an athlete of few words. Clark said, "I could not have chosen a better seatmate, medium sized and not disposed to conversation. Why I felt I should bear the social responsibility, I don't know.

"But it was a long flight. So I asked him the obvious—what sport was he in? He said, 'boxing,' without elaboration. When I inquired as to what weight class, he replied 'heavyweight.'

"Then I asked bluntly what was really on my mind, realizing that I was not indulging in social amenities at all but rather wanting to share my burden with this other Olympian, dark and dour.

"'Do you think you're going to win?'

"With a slow, broad smile, Joe Frazier said, 'I don't see any reason why not.'"

We were relieved when, after 12 hours, Japan came into view. Ted Nash, stroke of the four-without-coxswain, then went to the lavatory for awhile and emerged without his jacket, trimming down just to the polo shirt. He had pumped up his muscular arms with exercises and perhaps expected the Japanese media, upon our landing, to take notice and interview him, an Olympic medalist hero from 1960. After landing, Nash went unnoticed except by scorning teammates.

Buses took us to the Yoyogi Olympic village, a former U.S. military base which had been updated and amounted to a large complex with dining rooms and recreational facilities. We were to bunk on the second floor in rooms of three each. Bill Knecht, Chet Riley and I were together while Budd, still sick, got stuck with the Amlongs because everyone was still mad at him. Clark shared with Foley and Cwiklinski while Rosenberg, Zimonyi and Bill Donovan made up another trio.

The next morning our intent was to go to the course to rig our shell and test the waters of the Toda rowing course.

Bill Harahan, one of the team managers, described the outgoing 45-minute bus ride like this: "Rivaling the queasy emotions of a Cinerama roller coaster ride, the trip to Toda became a daily fantasy complete with a motorcycle escort and a loudspeaker-equipped police van which soundly rebuked stray motorists who inadvertently failed to yield the right of way.

"The stoic bus drivers acclimated to this procedure and anticipated complete subjugation to their right of way. The sight of petrified motorists frantically seeking safety for their vehicles on the sidewalks became a regular occurrence. The Czech and German oarsmen, too horrified to watch, buried their heads in their hands."

Coach Rosenberg decided that we would make only one such trip a day, remaining at the course for lunch, a nap and the second workout.

A perfect rowing course requires that all lanes have identical depth, at the least six feet of water below, and no current that might provide one crew or the other of the six an advantage—or a disadvantage—in a short six-minute race of 220 strokes or so.

The shores had to be graded so that backwash, waves rebounding off those shores, cannot corrupt a crew's track. A perfect course will also have introductory lanes for boats to row up to the start, then the six identical racing lanes 2000 meters to the finish line, with more meters for a run-out at the end. The only non-racing boat on the course is the launch containing the judge and a driver.

Thomas Keller of Switzerland, the president of F.I.S.A. therefore rowing's executive leader and also a sculler of note, mentioned to the Japanese that the wash from this launch was not being absorbed by the banks, that there was a kickback of waves causing interference problems.

Authorities promised Keller a resolution. The following morning we were astonished to see a burlap retaining wall, a Japanese "curtain in the water" measuring a mile and a quarter in length that had been constructed of effective burlap to absorb small waves. Several hundred men had worked all night to construct this wall. The Toda rowing course was ready and perfect.

We were pleased to find that the John B. Kelly, our shell, had arrived safely from Philadelphia, ready to be uncrated and rigged. A newer version, to be sent from Italy, had not arrived but we were comfortable rowing in the JBK that had got us here.

Our boat house was at the end of the course, about 2,200 meters from the starting area. This was the Hitsobashi University's big boat house where we had dressing rooms and a place to hang out. We were on the third floor, the French on the second. The toilets amounted to a hole in a porcelain basin where we stood, or squatted, and hoped for the best.

Emory Clark said, "This was easy enough to manage for Asian citizens, used to squatting on their heels when doing their business, but awkward for hulking Americans. Emptying out before a workout or a race is a significant part of every oarsman's pre-row ritual. We coped."

The Amlongs of course had distracting complaints. I ignored them.

At the Olympic Village we were assigned to eat with the English, Canadians and Australians. The tasty food—steak, potatoes, ice cream, salads without limitation—caused coach Rosenberg to say after a few days, "You better let up or you are going to eat yourselves out of a medal."

We peeked in the other dining rooms and scoffed at the pasta Italians, the wine French and the Japanese eating who-knew-what.

The Americans' food was prepared under the watchful eyes of Herman Rausch, the executive chef at the renowned Greenbriar resort in West Virginia.

Lack of nutrition was never a problem and I, a glutton, had the other eight of my crew watching me and denying me the second dessert, the best one.

Although the Olympic village had all sorts of evening entertainment I had on blinders—no socializing with the enemy, no trading pins or clothing with athletes from unknown shores. Solitude was how I concentrated. I was not interested in making new friends. I can recall nothing of life before the races. Reading usually was my escape.

We didn't see the Russians around but we were looking for them.

At the time, our overly concerned American crew was struggling to become healthy enough just to get on the water for any kind of a practice and regain the peak we reached before Budd's illness. Fortunately we were far from being overtrained.

At the time of the Tokyo Olympics many thought the athletes from the Communist countries were professionals paid by the state and thus exceeding the amateur athletic standards embraced by most international Olympic committees. The Soviets were cheating, it was said and written.

I felt this was unfair and that we should examine our own standards before being so critical of the Russians. Our athletes were represented as sacrificing rather than being coddled. I asked some of those most vehement on this subject, "Name one American athlete who has defected to the Soviet Union because the athletes are treated better there and have advantages over ours." The answer was always thoughtful silence.

The concept was that the struggling amateurs from the capitalistic countries deserved sympathy for overcoming so much. Time marches on. In the four decades since Tokyo the strict amateur codes have disappeared and the games are open to all. Furthermore American winners of gold medals in rowing each receive a prize of $25,000 from the United States Olympic committee.

As for the millionaire athletes in sports like basketball or tennis, I find it difficult to fault those who choose not to compete in the Olympics when they in effect would have to take a huge cut in salary and risk injury. The original ideals of the modern games have been so compromised they barely exist. But that is a soapbox for another time.

We had a habit of describing those who competed for the Soviet Union as Russians without making any distinctions. We were so wrong, ignoring the fact that they did not even share the same languages. There was silent resentment among many when they marched in the Olympic parades under the red hammer & sickle flag or, when on the medal stand, the Soviet national anthem was played. Back then such countries as Lithuania, Estonia, Latvia, Belarus, Ukraine, Georgia and many more, not free of the old U.S.S.R., had no national identity.

The Soviet championships and trials were won by Lithuania, but Communist approved Russians replaced several members of the eight when it was feared they might defect.

It was also false to claim that the Soviets, by having so many had military professionals in their sporting ranks, enjoyed an edge. What few realized was the size of the military contingent on the U.S. team. Almost one-fourth of that team was athletes on "special assignment," or as the Navy called it, "Temporary Additional Duty" from their regular duty, receiving full pay from the government while throwing the javelin or pulling on an oar. And more than one-fourth of the U.S. medals were won by those from that contingent.

At that time most healthy American males were subject to conscription. You could say that without being given the opportunity to compete many of those athletes in the service, in the prime years of their athletic prowess, would have lost the chance to represent their country in the Olympics.

I regarded this policy as being good public relations for the U.S. at a time when the Vietnam War was heating up and also controversy about it. I never knew of any athlete who joined the armed forces in order to compete but perhaps it happened.

There was nothing so new about this policy. Historian Andy Webb, a former coxswain at the U.S. Coast Guard Academy, has written, "American military personnel first competed in the Olympics at Stockholm in 1912 following Congressional authorization for soldiers to participate in the modern pentathlon (shooting, fencing, swimming, riding, and running) as well as in equestrian events. First Lieutenant George S. Patton represented the U. S. in that modern pentathlon."

In the 1950's, with the draft still in place, public laws were passed enabling military personnel to train for and compete in the Olympics. Of the 31 athletes on the American rowing team, eight were detached from active duty and I was one of the eight.

We all benefited early in the games at Tokyo when Billy Mills, a Marine Corps officer, won the 10,000-meter run. First Lieutenant William M. Mills of Coffeyville, Kansas, had taken up running to get in shape for boxing while attending a school for Native American orphans. Mills made for a wonderful media story.

While training at Vesper on leave from the Navy I had as a club mate the young John Lehman who later became the Secretary of the Navy. He was a supporter of military athletes, in part based on his experiences as a junior member of his uncle Jack Kelly 's Vesper Boat Club.

Navy LTJG Bill Stowe was one of many military personnel that represented the United States in Tokyo. Here his commanding officer, CDR. Wolfe inspects the gold spoils of victory.

Taking time off for the Olympics did not enhance one's military standing, however. Joe and Tom Amlong were examples of men whose promising careers were compromised as they found themselves passed over for advancement in rank. Joe jokingly said of Tom, "He had more Passovers than most rabbis."

In order to stay in the Air Force, and accumulate the 20 years needed for retirement as a captain, Joe had accepted a reduction of his rank down to sergeant.

He might have had a problem too, coming from an incident at an Equal Employment Opportunity seminar. He publicly challenged the black officer leading the group on the sexual prowess of the black race relative to his own libido. This event would be taken in stride by those who knew Joe, but it did not sit well otherwise.

We got a boost when Dietrich Rose, our rigger whom we needed, was given credentials to become an official member of the U.S. team based on the appeal that the equestrian team had horse groomers that were not Americans. Rose, along with the groomers, was accepted but he lacked the uniforms.

No problem. Dietrich easily befriended Dick Dunham, a dedicated and generous Olympic rowing personage who had access to the supplies. Soon Dietrich had his U.S.A. uniforms, parts of which he traded for multinational clothing that he wore for many years after Tokyo.

The best trading item of all was the 10-gallon cowboy hat, the symbolic imprimateur of President Lyndon B. Johnson which Rose parlayed into numerous German or Swiss sweatsuits. Dietrich also became our spy.

While riding a motor scooter up and down the race course, scouting crews and taking times, Rose gathered hints about race strategies that he fed to our seven crews—the eight, two fours, two pairs and the single scull.

Harvard's Harry Parker, the small boat coach, said, "Dietrich was so helpful. He and I went up that damn race-course bike path on scooters perhaps a thousand times. Sometimes he drove and I coached and other times I drove and he coached. We were at the course twelve hours a day."

Budd was back in the boat, but we had lost speed. Our 500-meter pieces were in the 1:24 range and we knew the Ratzeburgs were rowing faster, 1:22. Our new boat from Italy arrived and we hoped it would speed us up enough to be a contender. It had a name, "The Doc Riggall" after our old-time club president.

The weather was cool yet wet, our gear never dry. No dryers or space to hang the sweats. Chills led to grumpiness and to colds. Spirits were not great but with Boyce coming around we felt optimistic. We began to regain the lost speed.

Then, when everything was falling into place, Stan Cwiklinski was taken to the Olympic village's hospital with the flu.

29

Another Hurdle Before Gold

"It was the worst possible point in my life," remembered Stan Cwiklinski of the early days in Tokyo. "I don't know where I got it but I had the flu and it was like going through hell. It hit me soon after we arrived. I didn't tell anyone because I didn't want to upset anyone or deny myself the opportunity to row. So I tried to work it out alone as I felt that I had no where to turn.

"I finally came to terms with myself and I had to tell Allen that I was sick, really sick. I was shaking with fever. I confessed to Allen, I really don't recall how. But I wound up with the team physician, Dr. Dan Hanley from Bowdoin College, who gave me the death knell when he said 'Hey, you are done.'

"I told the doctor that I did not believe him. I yelled at him, 'I can't be done. I gotta get well, get over this, and get back in it.'

"There were eight days until our first heat. I spent two days in bed in the Olympic Village infirmary, in quarantine. There is not much you can do with a virus except take aspirin, a lot of liquids, and let it run its course.

"Dr. Hanley was not very conciliatory and he had an awful bedside manner. He said, 'There is no way I can put you back to health, to full status. You have got to succumb.'

"We did not get off on the right foot with this at all because I was not taking his premise it was over for me. I wasn't going to accept that."

Cwiklinski went on. "I felt that I had really let the team down. I was all alone attempting to sort this out, sicker than a fucking dog with a fever of 102 degrees, wondering how I was going to deal with this.

"I had no visitors in the infirmary until the second night. Conn Findlay came to see me. He said, 'I guess that I am risking catching this from you. But I am here to tell you—don't give up. I think you can get back.'

"Here was my hero, a gold medal winner taking the time to come and give me a pep talk. I don't know how he even knew that I was in the infirmary. There he was. He sat down next to my bed and I can't remember his words. But he gave me huge motivation to get going—to get out of the bed and get well.

"I will forever be indebted to Conn for this, the turning point in my sickness. While it wasn't easy, the fever began to break.

"The next day Al Rosenberg came to see me and he said, 'Look champ, we have to talk. I have Chet Riley in the boat. But I am not giving up on you. When do you think you can come back?'

"I told him that I would like to try right now, today. But Al told me to give it another day and then he would give me a shot at rowing in the boat again.

"Al said, 'Tomorrow we're going to row 500 hard strokes. I will put you in and your position in the boat will depend on how the boat goes. But with the race coming up so soon a decision has to be made.

"'If you can do it you will be in. Otherwise I'll have to go with Chet Riley.'

"I did not sleep too well knowing that it was all on the line for me in the morning. I will always be grateful to Allen for giving me a chance to prove myself again."

Now it seemed that Vesper was simply numb—numb to problems we appeared unable to avoid. First Boyce sick, now Stan, the constant abrasions coming from the Amlongs, the worrisome breaking-in of our new boat.

In Clark's log of October 4 he wrote, "Today Stan is sick with a cold or virus or something and Chet will row in his place. My attitude hits extremes regularly. Sometimes I think we are going to blow it like the Phils. Other times I think we are going to be in there." While we were in Tokyo the Philadelphia Phillies were losing their seven-game first-place lead in the National League, falling out of pennant contention.

Clark went on. "I guess that I am too sensitive, but it doesn't seem like ours is the way an Olympic effort ought to be. As Foley said, 'It's agony to row with Tom.' The agony that Foley speaks of gives me a headache, a physical thing. Because my thoughts are too unkind, and it's impossible to concentrate on anything else, the only cure is sleep.

"Oh well, the idea now is to keep my mouth shut, do my best, not let it get to me. Pray..."

On October 7, we carried our eight across a levee and away from the congested Toda course into the Arakawa River where we had a long, uninterrupted practice. Rosenberg had secured a launch and we were happy to row more than a mile and a quarter without having to turn around.

We rowed first with Stan in the boat and then Riley for a comparison. The times were equal. The decision had to be made that day based on our last hard workout before the upcoming first Olympic race.

Perhaps Riley was stronger but the cohesion was better with Stan and we assumed that his strength would return. Rosenberg talked to everyone in the boat separately gathering the confidence of each of us before making his decision. I thought that if all seemed equal we should go with Stan who earned his seat at the trials. Our final strokes that day were good and we did some starts rowing 52 strokes per minute.

The decision was made to race with Stan Cwiklinski in the three seat.

Chet Riley had been the perfect alternate. Had we raced with him finally he would not have adversely affected our performance. He was ready to go when called and gracefully stepped back when it was not essential for him to row.

When I talked to him about this almost four decades later, he said, "Stan earned the seat and deserved to row. I had a tight feeling in the pit of my stomach about replacing him for the actual racing and was prepared to do that.

"But I was not disappointed when he regained his health and I was off the hook. I think I did my job and earned my keep. It was a thrill to be such a close member of that great effort." Of course we were indebted to Chet Riley. But with Cwiklinski back we were back on track, regaining momentum with every practice stroke.

Rumors about the other crews spread and Dietrich Rose, our spy with a stop-watch, kept us informed about competitors' times and practices. There were eights from 14 countries entered and thus the competition would begin with three heats, two with five boats and one with four. The winner of each heat would qualify for the championship race embracing six crews.

Understand that there was a blind draw, meaning chance as to who would row whom in the first round, rather than some subjective seeding based on past performances. So it seemed possible that all the best boats could be in the same first heat, facing elimination if one or the other did not place first.

In order to minimize this possibility the eleven non-winners of the first heats would have a second chance and they would not have to row against the same boats they had raced in the first heats. In rowing these second-chance races are called a repechage, a French word. The three winners of the repechage races would then join the winners of the three opening heats for a grand final October 15, after a day off on the 14th.

We drew the greatly feared West Germans, the rabbit fast Yugoslavians, a good Italian boat and an untested eight from Australia. The second heat consisted of Czechoslovakia, Canada, Japan, New Zealand and Cuba while the four-boat third heat had the Soviet Union, Egypt, France and Korea. It looked like our heat was the toughest, and only the winner of the heat would advance directly to the final, the others to the repechage race in two days.

While our competitors had reached peak condition and confidence—and were attempting to hold at that plateau—our illnesses, delays, and other problems made it unclear whether we were arriving at our best. We were, however, on an upswing, gaining both speed and confidence.

30

Tension, Tension, Tension

With three long days until our first race, we became tense. Each of us handled personal emotions and acute stresses in some comforting manner yet never understanding why others didn't react in an identical fashion. I knew what was best for me and I didn't care what the others did as long as they left me alone.

Much is written currently about athletes and their "focus," a term that is apt for high-board divers but overused for oarsmen. You don't have focus about pulling an oar. That can cause a crab which will lose a race. The word has no meaning for me. When I was race rowing I had blinders on, as to what was going on around me. Maybe that's what focus is supposed to mean.

Although ours is the ultimate team sport the concentration subjects of each man in the boat will vary considerably. With our odd, sometimes ugly boatload of characters I'd say it remained best not to know how the others were coping. We just did our individual bits to prepare mentally for our time "all together."

You won't get from me any reflections of the initial pageantry of the Tokyo Olympics—opening parade, fireworks, hoopla—because I don't recall much about any diversions from the mission at hand. I possess total recall of the events following our racing. But under the veil of "focus" I don't have much remembrance of what went on before, my mind curled in a cocoon of concentration on the upcoming competition.

For example my parents had traveled from New York to watch but I refused to meet with them until after the racing was over. They understood.

The Amlong brothers must have been nervous because they mellowed somewhat, the highest levels of obnoxiousness declining then ceasing. They quickly befriended a weightlifting guru named Bob Hoffman, who convinced them that our performance would be enhanced if we took a host of non-prescription pills that he was marketing through his York Barbell Company in Pennsylvania.

In a nightly ritual the brothers would show up in our rooms with dirty handfuls of various colored pills, some as large as a quarter, and they expected us to drink them down. The big one would never have made it down my throat. Rather than argue, we accepted them with the promise that we would take them before going to sleep. But they wound up in the night table drawer and by the end of the games the drawer was full up.

The pills were left for the Japanese cleanup crew to ponder, even to report about what the Americans were up to. I never found out the ingredients of the pills and was pleased I never swallowed one. I suppose they were harmless herbal vitamins.

In 1964 there was no testing for performance-enhancing drugs and we knew nothing of steroids or blood doping. Because of mutual distrust of the Amlongs as dispensers of these pills or otherwise, none of us gobbled them down.

We had light practice rows to use up time in the last few days. We fine tuned the new shell and with every practice stroke and we became more comfortable with ourselves. We came to know where we were on the course without having to peek sideways out of the boat. Those 2000 meters became differentiated by smells, by shadows or just by the feel of where we were. The night before our first race I tossed and turned, visualizing how all those distinctions would unwind one after the other.

We had discussed our race plan carefully, what we expected we should do and what our competition most definitely would do. After exploring different scenarios we decided to row our own race at between 36 and 37 strokes per minute following a start of 24 strokes at a cadence of about 45 per minute. We discussed the potential sprint near the end, just when and where to take it as dictated by where we'd be relative to the others at certain points on the course.

It was time to put it all on the line, a tired yet catchy phrase that for once was applicable to our situation. On race day, October 11, there was no wind and racing conditions were perfect. As I've said I ate little before races skipping any kind of training meal contrary to what nutritionists recommended. But I believed that a hungry dog was a mean dog and I wanted to be mean, even rabid, on the water. It worked.

Our boat rigger, Nelson Cox from Princeton University, had cleaned and polished our racing shell and we launched it half an hour before the race with solemnity and purpose. We were keyed for a top performance but did not know what to expect, how good we might be—or might not be. We were quiet, determined, frightened. We were up against the reigning Olympic champions from Ratzeburg.

31

First Heat, Race of Our Lives

Rowing up to the starting line our thoughts shifted from various inward concerns to perfecting our strokes in a thorough warm up. I was oblivious to people in the stands or to the races underway—happy to be warming up and getting over my impatience at waiting.

Our preference in the 20-minute warm up was to take at least 100 hard strokes at a full racing cadence. With other eights rowing up and down the Toda course, we chose to row in lane zero, the practice lane next to the racing Lane One, and we did not have room for anything except a light paddle warm up.

Near the starting line we had about 15 minutes for the exclusive use of Lane Two, to which we had been assigned by the draw. We took several practice starts in the direction we would soon be racing. That's always wise because the feeling in the boat differs between a headwind or a tailwind and you want to be comfortable with the setting in which you will soon be racing.

Instructions to the crews were barked in French, the official language of rowing. The F.I.S.A. officials started counting down the remaining minutes to the race so the five crews would be on time in reaching their starting positions, confirming the schedule of the regatta's rigid program. Thomas Keller, the president of the International Rowing Federation (F.I.S.A.), did not tolerate any deviations from his plan for the proper running of a regatta. Although a wonderful Swiss gentleman, his Germanic intolerance showed when things did not go exactly as he had envisioned.

"Cinq minutes," the Starter announced from his tower behind the starting floats. We had five minutes for our last drills. "Quatre minutes," as we turned back towards the starting area, our warm up complete as we each had broken a slight sweat. "Trois minutes," the Starter precisely announced as we approached the starting floats, each of which had a prone person to grab and hold the sterns of the shells in place as the coxswains lined up evenly to begin. "Deux minutes" and we were in place, ready in Lane Two, with the Italians aligning themselves off our left side in Lane One. To the right were the Australians and Yugoslavs in Lanes Three and Four. To our far right the formidable Germans were in Lane Five.

The people on the floats held the sterns firmly as the bows were lined up evenly across the course. There is even an official called the Aligner whose job it is to make sure the crews are even so the start will be fair for all. When the boats seemed ready, and after an approving signal from the Aligner, the Starter from his elevated platform called to each crew asking in French if they were ready

Italie, pret?

Etats Unis, pret?

Australie, pret?

Yugoslavie, pret?

Allemagne, pret?

As they were polled each of the coxswains signaled with a hand wave to the starter that his crew was ready. The start would come momentarily and I took several last deep breaths knowing that my oxygen would soon be depleted.

This was it, the real thing. No more imagining this scene, the one we had been waiting for. No stopping the clock now. No more timed practice distances.

Holding up a red flag, which he would wave down abruptly when he'd give the command to go in French, the starter was poised for the perfect start. At last came his words, "Etes vous prets? Partez!"

We were off.

Our usual method at starting the boat was one stroke at three-quarters of the forward slide in our seats, just enough to anchor the blade by cramming down our leg drive and making a clean release. Then followed two halves of the slide to overcome the inertia of the shell. Next we pulled through three quarters of the slide again, and finally took a full stroke.

By then we were within our planned 20 quick strokes at a very high cadence before I brought down the stroke rate and settled for the body of the race. Those original short strokes are to get the boat up and moving. They do not put as much stress on the equipment or the oarsmen as if we were to take full strokes right from the word go. Partez!

All seemed well as Robby yelled for us to breathe on the fifth stroke. It is possible for oarsmen to forget to breathe in the first charge of battle, seriously endangering themselves with an oxygen depletion that they could not recover from. We had come off with a clean start and were in good position as we settled after twenty-five strokes into a normal racing cadence. It was our intention to row our own race, within ourselves, and not be concerned with our position in relation to the other boats.

Oarsmen are not supposed to look out of the boat during the competition for numerous reasons, the primary one being that they will lose their concentration on their own stroke and style. A crew has to do things in unison—all together—and wandering eyes cause wandering thoughts about the cadence or extra power strokes. The crew must follow the stroke with all the strength and guts it can muster.

By the five hundred meter mark we were still thrashing the water with fresh muscles and strength. Zimonyi informed us that we were a quarter length ahead of the crews on our immediate left and right. As expected the "fly and die" Yugoslavians were ahead but that was not our concern. The Germans were too far over to the right for us to see them even peripherally. Three minutes into the race—at the half way point—Zimonyi announced that we were even with the Germans which seemed to me to be a lie since I could feel that they were ahead. But not by too much.

I thought to myself, "They can be caught."

The water was being ferociously churned by the five boats as we proceeded. Only the Australians had fallen behind and out of contention. There was no time to think, no time to analyze, nothing to do but give it your best shot on every stroke, concentrating on not holding back—giving full power and calling on your reserves.

At the 1,500 meter mark we had pulled ahead of the others and were about a quarter of a length behind the Germans—less than one second back. We did not have enough left for a high stroking sprint since we had given our all to get where we were. We had rowed almost the entire course at above 38 strokes per minute, one or two strokes higher than our normal cadence. Even without a sprint we were closing on the Germans.

Alas, we finished second to the defending champions. It had not been our plan to sprint near the end, so we did not. That was the best we could do on this opening day of the rowing at the Tokyo Olympics. We had lost by 28/100ths of a second, or about three feet. Only 36 inches kept us from defeating the world champions, who had won in a fast time of 5:54.02.

Dejected, we paddled into the slip and were met by an ecstatic Jack Kelly. He told us what a great race we'd just rowed. Then an equally joyful Allen Rosenberg told us that we had won in effect. What is he talking about, I thought, we all thought. We'd lost and losing is terrible.

"No, no," he said, "You have won the right to win the final. And you are going to do it. That race was perfect. You have them set up for a loss in the final."

I thought both of them were nuts. We were so exhausted that it was a chore to get the boat out of the water and into the boat house. We barely managed to pose for a judges' picture, one to insure that we did not substitute a fresh oarsman into subsequent races. There were no smiles from the Vesper group as we posed but the Americans—except those that rowed—were upbeat and smiling. We were too tired and dejected by not crossing that finish line first.

Walking back from the finish line we were joined by Dr. Wolfe, our testing physician from the Valley Forge Heart Institute in Pennsylvania. He stopped us, gathered us around and said that we only rowed to 70 per cent of our capacity. One percent more and we would win the final.

Whaaaat!

I thought he had a lot of nerve telling us that we had more to give. Then he directed our attention to the German crew, whose boat was still in the water. It was 15 minutes after the race by then, and some of the Ratzeburg boys remained in the shell. Others were lying on the dock writhing, and some standing around as if in shock. Dr. Wolfe told us that we had absolutely rowed them out, that they had punished themselves too much and that they could not duplicate their effort again in this regatta. He then announced his prediction to us—we would beat them in four days and win the Olympic gold.

I began to absorb what he was saying, to take heart in the effort that we had just made. We'd rowed our race for what a first heat is and how it must be raced—well but with thought for another day, another chance. I kept in mind also that we had two men, Stan and Boyce, who were getting stronger day by day. In four days we would be that much better.

Next we were told that our time (5:54.30) was 12 seconds faster than the Russians (6:06.15) in their heat, and nine better than the winners of the third heat, the Czechoslovakians (6:03.88). Suddenly I did not feel quite as tired. I began to anticipate, even look forward to a re-row with the Germans. First, of course, we had to win our repechage to gain entry into the final, and anything can happen in a boat race.

32

The Repechage

The open draw, as who would race whom in the opening heats of the eights, did result in the fastest crews, ourselves and the Germans as it turned out, by chance rowing against one another. By winning that opening heat, the Germans advanced directly to the final set for October 14 while we had to row once more.

The second-chance system, the wonderful repechage, gave all the crews who did not place first in their heats another opportunity to qualify for the championship final among six boats. To get there you had to win your race.

We found that in our repechage we would be racing against eights representing Japan and Korea which had been 22 and 52 seconds slower respectively than our time of 5:54.30 in that opening heat. The fairness of the repechage is that we did not have to race the two other crews that had placed second, Canada or France or the crews that we had already defeated in our heat, Yugoslavia, Italy and Australia.

We assumed that it would be a cakewalk. We relaxed and looked forward to that race as a tune-up for the final and as an all-together crew at last we were of one mind about this.

Eyes had been opened by our performance against the Germans and we were regaining the confidence that we'd had prior to losing to them. I supposed that rowing buffs the world over were riveted to our rowing in Tokyo and was not so surprised when I was approached at dinner in the Olympic Village by a reporter who identified himself as representing the Associated Press.

He said, "Bill, do you have a minute to talk with me?"

The other Vespers, with eyebrows raised, were impressed that this reporter would seek me out and know my name. They were all ears as the interview commenced. He asked how I liked the Olympic Village, something about the food, and who did I think the major struggle for the gold would be with?

I responded, "The Russians are strong and really stand between us and gold."

He carefully recorded that in his note book. My teammates were agreeing with my answers and were in awe of my interview that would be in major American newspapers the next day. All went well until he asked me about my free throw percentage.

I answered quizzically, "Free throw percentage?"

"Aren't you Bill Bradley, the basketball player?"

I answered, "No, I'm Bill Stowe, the oarsman."

Thereupon he slammed his notebook shut, muttered, "Oh shit," as he arose and left the table. Poor interview manners, I thought, especially for a disciple of the Associated Press.

The Vespers guffawed over the misidentification and enjoyed my discomfort. I had the last laugh in that Bradley, the Princeton luminary to become a star with the champion New York Knickerbockers of the National Basketball Association and an United States Senator, looked like me—not me like him.

In our race to qualify for the final it was our plan to work on the best possible start, then cruise through the middle of the race, simply holding our position. We'd take the last 500 meters with a good solid sprint as practice for the final. We had no pressure upon us by any reckoning, and only a stupid mistake or an act of god could cost us a place in the final. Mistakes happen but against the Japanese and Koreans it would have to be a major catastrophe. We had a lot of comfort room and it would take more than hitting a buoy, a seat jumping out of its slide or someone catching a minor crab to disrupt our required first place.

Even my parents decided that it was not going to be much of a race and took a tourists' day excursion away from Tokyo and this rowing foolishness.

We believed that we owned this race but the Japanese thought differently and had nearly 25,000 spectators lining the banks to witness their day in the rising sun of grand expectations.

Clark wrote in his log, "Few of those spectators heard the blood curdling 'bonsai' with which the Japanese boat took its first stroke. Or saw them jump the start (also called stealing the start, meaning going off before the Starter said go, or partez.) Had it not been so serious it would have been funny and I almost smiled as we got underway, waiting for the referee to call the false start. Which he did not.

"I forgot for a moment that we were in Japan. The host nation has its prerogatives. So with 20 strokes gone, we found ourselves a good half length behind and the Japanese rowing their normal brisk 52 strokes per minute. No one panicked as we stuck to our race plan which was to drop the stroke to 34 for the middle thousand meters and then at the 1500 meter mark, regardless of where anyone was, kick it up as high as we could to work on our sprint.

"In any event, we caught and passed the Japanese in that first 500 and took it down on cue to slug it out at the unfamiliar and uncomfortably heavy low stroke in the middle 1000 meters of the course.

"Coming up to the stands and the biased crowd, it must have looked like the Japanese had a chance for an upset—we had only about a length on them—as we were greeted by a great roar. By that time we had forgotten about the other boat and just wanted to get it over. So we took the stroke up and moved out to three lengths of open water on the Japanese right in front of the stands. It must have looked as if we were pouring it on, which is not what we intended as we were thinking of the Germans with every stroke."

The U.S. finished the race way ahead. Apparently no offense was taken as the Japanese were courteous. Their stroke and captain presented us with Admiral Togo's Imperial Navy pennant from the victorious 1904-05 war against Russia, a sincere gesture of good luck for the finals. For them, the honor in a defeat was to see the winner go all the way.

The race was a good outing, a diversion kept us from going stir crazy, a workout we needed to get better and boost our confidence. We were putting more and more distance between our problems and our goals.

During the day off before the final we had a light workout of three short 250-meter sprints. The boat was ready and going great. It was time to put it to bed before the big day.

33

The Wait

Waiting for a big race is an excruciating experience as time goes so slowly, resigning an oarsman to his singular thoughts. I don't remember much about the 24 hours before the race and I doubt I was a nice person as I stumbled around. My leave-me-alone attitude enveloped me and I was alone under a veil of concentration. Even the invidious Amlong brothers seemed to disappear. I was persuaded they too were so wrapped up in personal thoughts as to overlook their roles as agitators.

It was impossible to sleep the night before the final and I was furious for robbing myself of what I thought was needed rest, or even some subconscious mode of relaxation.

I tried everything to ditch the misery of my repetitive thoughts—the race playing over and over. It would not go to rest and counting sheep didn't work either. Eating was out of the question, except perhaps for some tea and toast. Race day? I have no recollection until the actual race itself.

While the Vespers were absorbed in their fate others on the U.S. rowing team had their own problems. The most serious came in the four-without-coxswain from Seattle when Phil Derbrow ruptured his congested sinus during the opening heat. Six-foot three and 190 pounds, this talented oarsman was in the three seat right behind Ted Nash, the stroke and catalyst of this tough talented crew.

Nash described what happened: "We were ahead of Great Britain at the 1000-meter mark and the boat was comfortably flying when Phil coughed and spit blood on and over my right shoulder.

"The boat slowed and Phil said 'I'm O.K. Let's go.' But he had a second episode of blood loss and the guys in the bow, who could see his condition, said to me, 'Phil's really hurting. Please paddle.'

"We did and still took second by three lengths or more. Phil went to the hospital by ambulance and we were not allowed to see him in intensive care for several days."

Dan Hanley, the U.S. team doctor, said that Derbrow would not row again in the games because he could bleed to death internally if he had another rupture. No one could dispute that.

A major injury like this one, when occurring in such a preliminary race, sanctions the substitution of another oarsman and the replacement for Derbrow was Geoff Picard, the team spare from Harvard who had filled in for us when Boyce Budd was sick with mononucleosis.

Nash said, "Phil Derbrow was one of the strongest men I have ever rowed with and we really felt that we were on our way to the gold. Picard did a great job in replacing him but with our different West Coast style and rhythm he never totally fell in synch."

The Vesper group had grown to like Picard while having less compassion for prideful Ted Nash. To needle Nash we called the new lineup The Picard Four. After only one practice, with Picard the replacement, this crew won its repechage, went to the final and captured third, becoming Olympic bronze medalists.

Our race morning was cool and overcast. Not a day to remember for wonderful weather. In the Olympic Village we noticed the wind kick up a bit but the Toda race course was miles away. We watched the first race out there on television and were not surprised when the Germans won the four-with-coxswain as they were the defending Olympic champion and had posted the best time in the opening heats.

Startling to us was that in the order of finish the gold medal winner had rowed in lane six, the silver medal winner in lane five, and the bronze in four. The fourth place crew had come from lane three, the fifth in two and the sixth and last in lane one.

We deduced that the quartering headwind from the northeast was brisk and provided a sheltered advantage to the lanes furthest from the grandstands.

The second championship race of the day provided a surprise in that it was won by two Canadians who had come to Tokyo as spares for their eight. George Hungerford and Roger Jackson had hardly been favored. It was immediately claimed the wind force had helped them as to rowing in an advantaged lane.

The always reliable official guide of the N.A.A.O. reported in its annual wrap up, "This was probably the most controversial race of the regatta because the cross wind gave substantial shelter to lane six and progressively less to the others. In later races the wind shifted to a steady headwind and subsided somewhat for the eights."

In defense of the Canadian pair-without-coxswain they did have the fastest time in the heats and the stir about their victory was undeserved, say I.

Then it was announced the races would be suspended until the wind died or shifted direction, and in the Olympic Village we were told to wait, delay setting out for the course until further notice. Not a happy decision for keyed athletes. We had no idea of the politics that went on at Toda leading to the unprecedented stoppage of the races and later I learned of them.

Harry Parker, the assistant U.S. coach responsible for the small boats, was incensed that the finals had continued under unfair conditions in his opinion. He accosted Tommy Keller, the F.I.S.A. chief, and insisted the races be delayed, halted immediately.

Parker told me 37 years later in the Harvard Boathouse, "I'm the guy who went screaming and hollering to Keller that we had to postpone the races. I just hated to see crews racing in unfair conditions like that and I had protested even before the regatta began.

"After wins in lane six in the first two races, I went to Keller and said, 'Did you see that? You're responsible for that. You will have this on your head for the rest of your life. How can you run races in these conditions?'

"Others pulled me away from further confrontation and I ran to the boathouse and told our pair, Conn Findlay and Ed Ferry, not to launch because the water was so rough.

"Conn looked at me and said, 'You better know what you're doing because if they start the race without me you're dead.'

"I still told them not to go out there and I went back to Keller and told him that I am not putting the American boats on the water. Finally they decided to hold the races up, and after two hours the wind direction shifted and the still strong wind came directly down the course. That made it fair for all. Early on it was terrible."

My first thoughts decades later, after hearing Harry Parker tell me his story, was to view him as heroic in taking such a strong stance against the domineering Keller. Parker, then a young coach with little renown, had on his own brought the regatta under control.

After further consideration I realized that our Vesper eight had stood to gain advantage because our assigned lane was wind favored. Parker had done us no favor by having the regatta halted. Do I take the credit away?

No. As it turned out we didn't need any help and I am glad that the course was deemed fair for our own race. At the time, however, I would have taken any advantage, regardless of how unfair, in order to win.

When it was announced that the races would commence again, we departed the Olympic Village two hours behind schedule. We arrived having survived a final harrowing bus ride. The bus driver and the police escort felt ever more important and were determined to get us to the Toda race course rapidly at any cost. Agitation we did not need.

In our locker area we tried to get some rest on the provided tatami mats. The races were postponed again and we worried that the races would not get off that day. A delay of a day would have compromised the Olympic schedule, which had the canoe and kayak races beginning at Toda following our races, and upset the television programming. More important a postponement would be a disaster for our psyches.

While we were cloistered in our waiting room, Dietrich Rose made one last check of our boat and discovered that many of the nuts and bolts in the outriggers had been mysteriously loosened.

The angle of the oar's blade when it enters the water is critical and is determined by the angle of the containing oarlock, which is adjustable by those nuts and bolts in the supporting triangular metal brace we call an outrigger. Without getting too technical, the perfect angle of the blade in relationship to the surface of the water is nine degrees upon entry, seven degrees when the oar is perpendicular to the direction of the shell, and four or five degrees at the finish of the stroke. Any deviation from this formula can render the bladework ineffective.

Our outriggers had been modified—abused evilly—and Dietrich's vigilance saved us from disaster. While the Olympic boat house shared by all the crews was patrolled by security guards some authorized figure could have tampered with our boat. There were no accusations and no approach to authorities. Dietrich quietly set the riggers right and did not divulge the incident until afterward.

During those upsetting delays I can only imagine what was going on in the locker rooms of our competitors. We were ready even though the delay and wait were difficult. An overtrained or wound-up crew might have more trouble with the race delay than one not working so close to frazzled nerve ends.

The Japanese were so accommodating to their Olympic visitors, so desirous that everything be perfect. The delay of the finals was an embarrassment to the organizing committee but outside of their control caused by an act of nature, wind.

Yushi Nakamura, long an important figure with the Japan Rowing Association, described to me what went on behind the scenes while we oarsmen waited. The hosts, he related, were concerned not so much about the delays effecting the course schedule the next day but more so of a social event. The Japan Rowing Association had prepared an important after-the-finals goodbye for all at Chinzano, a famous and expensive garden party spot. A cancellation or a rescheduling was unthinkable, and the association's budget had been stretched by having to build that burlap wave-control curtain.

Then there was the impending darkness. Yushi Nakamura's account here is so sterling to my chronology. He related to me by mail while doing my research, "I have no exact memory but two or three races prior to the final of the eight it became dark and I saw many people gathered at the finish line attempting to shine automobile headlights across the course to assist the judges.

"Trouble was in those days photo film was not as fast as today and car headlights were not enough to shine across the 100 meters of the course at the finish. It would be fatal that the Japanese organizing committee could not record the result of the Olympic finals on film.

"Suddenly I got an idea. The Japanese Defense Forces had been deeply involved in the Olympic Games with their mobile electric power and equipment. At Toda they were present with the telecommunications equipment between the start and finish line and along the course. My idea was that perhaps they had a special tool to give enough light for our needs. Fortunately I was at the 2050 meter mark next to their headquarters van. I approached the senior officer and asked, 'Do you have any tool or equipment to help us?'

"He replied, 'We have star shells. They can illuminate the course like in daytime.'

"May we use them?

"His quick answer was yes.

"I called the F.I.S.A. headquarters to tell them that star shells were available and they were pleased. We carefully calculated the speed of the boats and set the timing of the shooting, then tried it in the last three races.

"For the eights grand final we planned to shoot one right as the crews passed the 1500-meter mark and a second one 45 seconds later. The star shells worked perfectly and we even had one left over to light up the medal presentation, giving a very dramatic scene."

Of course we oarsmen, the actors in this scheme, were unaware of such a state of affairs while hunkered down with our nerves in the waiting room. Rosenberg was fretting about our not having eaten and lacking the energy to race. We wanted to get it over with.

From Clark's log comes this: "Then, after another interminable time, Dietrich banged through the door with his usual subtlety saying, 'Let's beat those fucking Krauts.' With that Germanic exhortation we peeled off our sweats and headed for the boat."

34

The Gold Medal Race

There was a presentation stand and ceremony at Toda for the rowing victors, race by race. As we walked down to the boat house to do our business in something of a daze, the Star Spangled Banner played at the finish line to honor our pair-with-coxswain, Conn Findlay, Ed Ferry and Kent Mitchell, for taking this day's first American gold. Because the wind had shifted the issue of unfair lanes had been resolved and the regatta had resumed.

Boyce Budd and Emory Clark were of one contentious and conflicted mind having beaten the Findlay pair way back at the N.A.A.O. championships on the Schuylkill.

Clark had a trenchant recall: "As we in the eight took our boat off the rack, at that moment they carried theirs in—medals around their necks—and wished us luck. If ever I wanted to trade places with anyone, it was at that moment. Boyce and I had beaten them. Hadn't we?"

Launching a shell for the final race at any important regatta is a stoic occasion, one deliberate in its actions and the promise of let's-get-it-over-with.

After hand checking every nut and bolt with great care, we settled into our boat and its routine—to be pushed off and away from the dock to get out in the water so as to row. An inanimate eight-oared shell, its eight wings awaiting, is about to spring forth like a gaggle of geese taking off.

The convenient push comes from someone, anyone, on the dock and the place for the pushing hands is on the blunt ends of the oars, the tips. There is nothing special to this ancient accommodation.

Except that Jack Kelly, Allen Rosenberg and Dietrich Rose were there to do that, to push us off. For a silly instance I wished that they were in my place so I could have the comfort of watching the race instead of having to row it.

Without too much conversation or fanfare, we were pushed off and on our own. We had to row up the course in lane zero next to the judges' stand and the winners' dock and before the crowd of about six thousand. I was oblivious to all this as we inched along, out of the way of the double sculls final that was soon to be underway. That race would be using all six of the racing lanes.

Darkness was almost upon us and while the wind was still blowing, it appeared to be coming straight down the course. It favored no lane in particular and a headwind was pleasing to this former Cornell oarsman who had always won when there was one.

The headwind provides an advantage to longer stroking, and also to the bigger oarsmen whose weighty momentum and extra strength propel the shell into the wind. Lighter crews tend to drag when their oars are not in the water because of the wind resistance on the blades. High stroking crews are at some disadvantage as well because the oars are out of the water more often, the headwind pushing against them. At least that's the theory and I am not about to argue the point. I was happy, perhaps more than the others in the boat who had not experienced those cold headwinds whistling down Cayuga Lake at Cornell.

At about the 1000-meter mark on our way to the start we stopped rowing as the doubles race came by en route to the finish line. The American double of Sy Cromwell and Jim Storm was in a concentrated battle for the lead with the Russian duo. We attempted to shout encouragement to these friends who went on to win silver medals.

When we reached the starting area most of the other eights were on the line ready to go and we had time for only one practice start, but it was a good one. We were psyched up. The clock would not stop for us to ponder our preparation and we had to hurry to get into the starting position in lane six, the one furthermost from the grandstand and the finish-line judges.

The other five crews ranged off to our left, Germany in lane three and Russia in lane two. Yugoslavia floated in lane one, good because they could not divert our attention with their rabbity start, a distracting factor for a crew attempting to take control of a race at its own pace. Right next to us was the competitive eight from Czechoslovakia and one over in lane four Italy, not expected to mount any challenge. We were fortunate with our lane placement as we could concentrate on our own race and not be distracted by those from whom we expected the foremost challenges.

We did not have time to consider all this because the Starter was already polling the crews. Were we ready for the start? Being in lane six we were the last ones polled.

"Etats-Unis, prets?" said the Starter, followed quickly by "Messieurs, etes vous prets?"

Then came "Partez" and the race was on. In roughly six minutes it would be over.

Boyce Budd, recalling his thoughts, said, "I wanted to be thinking that I would tear up the course and row the race of my life. But I found myself getting in the boat and thinking instead where am I?

"What am I doing? Why did I ever get myself into this kind of position? Why can't I just be a normal human being watching the Olympics?

"The only way I could describe the pressure was the realization that quite soon I was going to give my all for something. Am I ready to do that?

"And the answer was no. I wasn't ready. I had lost control of my life. I'm now on a treadmill.

"I remember when rowing up the course something in the back of my head said, 'You've got to really pour it out on these practice starts. You got to get up a sweat by the time you're on the line. You've been through this before. You know that if you don't get your heart rate up, if you're not sweating by the time you get to the line you are not going to race your best race.' It was like a nightmare."

"We had gone up the course and it was very late in the afternoon, the light coming in on a flat angle. We got lined up, the worst moment in my life as an oarsman."

"And then we produced, by my book, the best start ever. I was amazed that there was hardly any of the usual smacking of puddles with water flying all over the place. It was one of the cleanest starts that I recollect us ever doing, with the high stroking we hoped for which only comes with clean bladework and perfect precision. I remember thinking we finally got this old ship rocking.

"But I was still on automatic and this was like an out-of-body experience. I was just doing what my body was trained to do. I was not telling myself to pull harder each stroke. I was just doing it."

After the start we settled into a long 37 strokes per minute. As planned we had not let anyone get away from us in the first minute. We were prepared, and expected, that the field might move ahead after the start. We knew the closer we could keep them, the easier it would be to pass them in the middle of the race.

We never wanted the competition to think that they could sit back with a lead on us, or in any way discourage us. We were cruising and comfortable rowing at our relatively low 36-37 strokes per minute in the steady headwind which produced a bit of a chop.

A minute into the race, Robby announced through his megaphone, "Vee are in third place." I clearly remember thinking if we could stop the race right here I would be happy with the bronze medal—without the gamble for the gold. But the race could not stop, and did not stop for me because I wished to accept third place.

According to the official split times taken at 500 meters, we were less than a second behind the high stroking Germans and just 12/100ths of a second behind the Soviet crew.

Our race plan called for us to take a power ten, a first extra-effort move, when we got our second wind. That was at about 800 meters. It would be followed by a surprise twenty more power strokes at roughly 1200 meters. By then we hoped to catch the field napping, struggling with the headwind and the more difficult water conditions.

The race fell in place for us. We were in good shape at the 750 meter mark. The lightweight Yugoslavian crew could not handle the rough water or the steady headwind and they fell to a surprising fifth, never to recover. The Italians were outclassed from the beginning, never a factor. It would be a race for the gold among the American, German and Soviet crews.

However the marvelous Soviet crew, the Lithuanians from Vilnius, rowed themselves out in the first 500 meters and could not recover. Thirty seven years later Antanas Bagdonavicius, the seven man, revealed that they had been instructed by their Russian Olympic team leaders to row for the gold and not to care about any other placement. All or nothing. They had been further hampered by illness and were not of physical size to handle the steady wind force against them.

By 1000 meters we had drawn to within five feet of the Germans or about ten feet closer than we had been in the regatta's opening heat at the same halfway mark. The Soviet crew had dropped back, out of contention.

Increasing darkness made it difficult to determine our position. However I could glimpse the white shirts with the black stripes that were the Germans. We were very close to being even, rowing well and with confidence.

Then came our second series of power strokes, at about 1200 meters, and we were flying. We took a seat with each stroke meaning we gained about four feet of additional advantage every time we put the oars in the water. We walked on the Germans.

From the stroke seat I could feel that the entire crew was pouring all they had into that special move designed to break the backs of those struggling to stay with us. We did it all together to a theme of total effort, everything we had.

And it worked.

At the end of the power twenty we had open water, more than a boat length lead on the world champion Ratzeburg eight and they were fading. It was a matter of holding on and trusting that we had shattered their spirit.

Only a calamitous mistake could still lose the race for us. Lo and behold, it almost happened.

Emory Clark recalls, "Just about then, as I was rowing along thinking how tired I was, my blade slapped a wave on the recovery and spun in my hands so that when I got to the catch that lovely cupped Karlish oar was backwards. I don't know how I knew it was backwards, but I did.

"Never having experienced that precise misadventure before, I did not know precisely what to do. Since we were rowing at 37 strokes a minute there was not a lot of time for mental debate.

"But I alertly concluded it would be unwise to put the oar in the water. So I pulled what the British call an 'air shot' and frantically twisted the oar handle around properly when it was in on my body. On my next trip up the slide, I decided the others could row it in.

"I was going to make sure I did not mess up, catch a crab or do something equally catastrophic. It was so dark I did not think anybody noticed—the boat kept on churning. But Robby said he saw it and Boyce claims he started to pray after sensing the missed stroke which he knew could only have been by his fellow Yalie.

"Life for all of us might have become different after that murky moment of high drama. It was one of those things that can make your palms sweat 37 years later."

With 500 meters to go we were in control of the race and as the stroke I made the decision not to take the cadence higher. Why risk a crab? We had shown our potential sprint ability in our repechage against the Japanese but did not need to risk it here.

There comes a point in a race when you know you have won it. Or at least should win it. This was the Olympic trials again. We were sitting on the Germans like we had the Harvard boys. Only a serious mistake could rob us of the gold that most of us had never really thought we could win. We still had sixty strokes to go into an abating headwind, approaching the lee shoreline of a totally dark Toda rowing course. Blackness lay beyond the finish line.

The regatta had been delayed for over two and a half hours by a seemingly unfair quartering headwind, a delay that put us in the race of our lives at night-time's drop. My night vision was enough to tell me that we had a comfortable lead. Yet you can never be comfortable until you are over the finish line.

The six thousand rowing fans were unable to make out the approaching boats until the Japanese Defense Forces shot off their first magnesium star shell into the sky. A floating illumination from the red flaring light began to cast an eerie glow over an incredible scene.

As we rowed "all together" for the last 500 meters those in the boat had different thoughts. Joe Amlong, up in the bow and out of coxswain Robby Zimonyi's earshot, remembers thinking, "It can't be this easy."

Joe further commented, "We were sitting out there in front of these guys and you are prepared to kill yourself. The call would never require it. The races you win are the easy ones, and the ones you lose are the harder ones. I think for that particular race I was ready to die before someone would go by me.

"At the start I always have butterflies and I pray to god I can hold out through the thing because I know it is going to hurt. In my mind I was ready to kill myself to win but I did not have to call up that type of courage. Everything was clicking just right."

Hugh Foley, also up in the distant bow, was confused when the parachute flares were launched to illuminate the course. He said, "When I heard the flares explode I remember distinctly thinking that someone had finished the race ahead of us. The race was over and we had gotten third.

"I couldn't hear Zimonyi and I could not see. I had worn glasses since I was in eighth grade and in those days they were heavy and I had left the black horned rim things on the shore. So it did me no good to look out of the boat because I couldn't see anything. Fortunately I did not stop rowing because we still had a minute left to row to the finish line."

From the three seat Stan Cwiklinski could hear Robby in the last 500 meters yelling, "Let's go boyz!! Vee are vinning! Vee are vinning!!"

But Stan did not believe him and simply pulled all the harder. He recalls, "I remember light coming in on the port side from headlights and the huge scoreboard, while there was total darkness off to the side where our competition was rowing. It was a surreal tunnel vision with light on one side and dark on the other. I was not sure what was happening but assumed that exhaustion was eating into my senses."

From the four seat, Tom Amlong could hear Zimonyi yelling, "Vee are vinning, vee are vinning." According to Tom, "It was just as big a shock to me as anyone. My idea of just making the Olympic team was all that I needed to complete my rowing career. If I made the team, I didn't give a hoot if I came in last.

"My mother asked me before I left for Tokyo, 'Do you think you have a chance?' I replied. 'Not a chance in hell.' It was a surprise to me right up until we crossed the finish line."

Clark, who had regained control of his oar and resumed rowing, said, "With 500 meters to go I was very much worried about a German sprint and not feeling much like sprinting myself. Then there was a bright explosion and another and I had something else for my ravaged brain to focus on.

"Could we have passed the finish line? Had I so miscalculated? But they don't shoot off guns at the Olympic finish and, spaced out though I may have been, I knew we had only rowed 1500 meters. Robby was probably saying something but he had lapsed into Hungarian again and I couldn't hear him anyway because of the new intermittent explosions of the launching flares.

"In any case it seemed prudent to keep on rowing. So I did and kept watching the Ratzeburgs who didn't seem to be coming on. I say 'seem' because it was all so surreal. The sky brightened considerably in a patchy sort of Fourth of July way and there was considerable noise from the stands, even though we were way across in the far lane.

"Crowd noise is always good in a boat race because, ahead or behind, it means you are going to get to stop rowing soon. While I felt it very worthwhile to keep an eye on those white shirts with the black stripe, I still was not thinking about winning.

"The gold, indeed, was a long way from my mind. Rather I was still very concerned about the possibility of having to sprint. I thought I could sustain the groove of pain I was in but was not sure I could crank it up to a more exquisite level. Well before it was proper, I began longing for the finish.

"And finally we stopped rowing. Since the Germans put in another four or five strokes, it seemed as though we had won. But it didn't matter. All the baloney about winning and losing could wait. I was only glad not to be rowing anymore."

The Olympic Champion Vesper Boat is a length and a quarter over the darkened finish line as Germany comes in second.

Still attempting to prove himself after his illness and absence, Boyce Budd pulled harder as to justify his position in the boat. He remembers, "The whole race was such a complete blur, everything so totally on automatic for me. The last 500 meters was a blizzard. I remember noise and confusion because we were rowing in the dark. And I remember the flares going up.

"Only I wasn't totally sure whether they were flares or the kind of flares that go off in your brain when you are totally out of control. I was so completely exhausted, I was just doing what I had been trained to do.

"I was just going up and down the slide. And I guess I was pulling. Then finally out of all this noise and confusion, as the crowd was screaming and we were beginning to pick up their sounds, I heard Robby say, 'You are vinning, you are vinning. You are the vorld champions.'"

Bill Knecht took his memories with him to his grave so I cannot produce a quote explaining his attitude during the final period of the race. He was a perfect seven man and exuded confidence. With more rowing experience than any others in the boat, he had known that this was his last shot at the Olympics. The victory was especially sweet for Knecht who kept a mental score of his life achievement contest with his good friend Jack Kelly. This was something that Kell could not get and for Bill Knecht a perfect time to retire from rowing.

Then, with 20 strokes to go, Zimonyi took his hands off the rudder lines and dipped them into the water, splashing me and yelling again, "Vee are the vinners!!" I resented his having the energy to be so happy. I still had over 100 meters to row and the celebration had to wait. We could still screw it up and rob ourselves of the highest pinnacle that any oarsman can achieve.

We were not there yet.

The end came in the dark at Tokyo without a special flourish. We were oblivious to the cheering or the spectators and coxswain Zimonyi never had to yell the cease rowing command, "Weigh enough!" We calmly stopped rowing, drifting away from the finish line under the quiet evening, into the pitch darkness. Five trailing boats did the same. We saw them back lit against the beams of light emanating from the grandstand, each of us immersed in personal thoughts too out of breath or tired to yell. Showboating was unnecessary. Nobody could see us anyway.

The race plan was well conceived by the coaching staff and perfectly executed by the crew. The conditions were to our liking and although Europeans do not favor headwinds I believe that it was a fair contest. I had experienced rougher times on some of their courses.

The Germans, good sportsmen all, never made any excuses for taking second and they made us feel like worthy champions. According to Karl VonGroddeck they simply rowed too hard in the first 1000 meters.

35

The Aftermath

The tranquility of exhaustion took over for these few minutes that followed the finish of the race in the dark. As we regained our breath, the enormity of the achievement began to seep in. Too tired to wave arms, hoot and holler, we drifted instead. Robby broke our moment of solitude by announcing that we had to go to the winners dock.

We had to get our medals.

We paddled to the dock where we were greeted by the exuberant trio of Kelly, Rose and Rosenberg. They had watched the race from the 1,500-meter mark where they witnessed the power twenty that cracked the race open, spewing forth the new world champions. Although still out of breath from running to the winners' dock they had not lost their exhilaration over the victory.

Avery Brundage, the president of the International Olympic Committee, stood on the dock and draped the medals over our heads one by one. He was followed by Thomas Keller who expressed congratulations on behalf of F.I.S.A.

Then came the wonderful, sentimental and even tearful moment for the national anthem to be played. It is every amateur athlete's dream to stand on that winners' platform as the undisputed best in the world. There is no greater high and it can endure for years.

Watching the Stars and Stripes being raised in the Tokyo night, from left to right, are Joe Amlong, Hugh Foley, Stan Cwiklinski, Tom Amlong, Emory Clark, Boyce Budd, Bill Knecht, stroke Bill Stowe, and coxswain Bob Zimonyi.

Getting back in the shell, we paddled away from the dock, making room for the Germans to be awarded their medals. The thrill was beginning to sink in and we waited on the water while the Ratzeburgers received their silver medals.

*Waiting in the darkness as the Silver and Bronze medals were awarded after
the final of the Olympic eights race.*

Then, surprisingly, the Czechoslovakians got out of their boat for their bronze
medals. They had beaten the Russians for third place. The huge electronic scoreboard posted the headwind slowed times as follows; 1st USA—6:18.23; 2nd Germany 6:23.29; 3rd Czechoslovkia 6:25.11; 4th Yugoslavia 6:27.15; 5th U.S.S.R
6:30.69; and 6th Italy 6:42.78.

The German boat, afterwards, rowed next to us in the dark and we exchanged
shirts, a very old rowing tradition.

It is not my intention to write in detail about the pomp and circumstance of
the Olympic games. Group dynamics has been the focus of this work, most interesting being the unholy alliance of Allen Rosenberg, Jack Kelly and Dietrich
Rose.

Together they were a force and the victory would have been impossible without their efforts for the good of the boat club and the goal of the Olympics. The
impossible happened by blending Kelly, the Philadelphia socialite and Irish Catholic jock, with the diminutive ex-coxswain Rosenberg and Rose, who had grown
up in Nazi Germany. We oarsmen were indebted to them.

Kelly had sought to continue the legacy his father had left him. He had found
a way to bring glory to the Vesper Boat Club in a most novel and exceptional

manner. Responsible for everything behind the scenes, he dealt with the club and the politics of amateur sport. He had dickered with the military in seeking the best oarsmen available. He dispensed the money. And he brought to the boat house the coaching that made Vesper far better than any standard that his father would have attempted.

I cannot say enough about the technical ability and forged wisdom of Allen Rosenberg. Simply stated, he was a terrific coach. Al was soft spoken and treated his athletes as equals, with respect. He not only told us what to do but why we were doing it. He had the crew believing in his methods which always happened to be right despite moments of dissent from Kelly.

Dietrich Rose handled all of the off-water training. As the captain of the club, he trained side by side with us. He had become an expert about rigging and handled the intricate details of a complex and different piece of equipment—the Italian built Donoratico eight-oared shell. Dietrich encouraged all of us, realized the weaknesses of the competition and kept us abreast of what was happening outside of our limited sphere of knowledge.

Kelly, Rosenberg, and Rose were just three of the 100 or so ingredients that went into the making of the Vesper victory. However that union of three minds comes first of all.

When we rowed with the American colors we represented the United States and had our country's support. We also had the backing of a traditional club that was no stranger to world class rowing. We were proud to be a part of Vesper and we all have life memberships, continuing to support the club's efforts. We represented those whom we left at home at 10 Boathouse Row and we felt their encouragement. In addition we had the backing of Philadelphia, a large city with the heart of a small town. Upon our return to Philadelphia we were treated as local heroes and that too was gratifying.

When in Tokyo I personally felt that we were also representing all those 15 crews we had raced at the trials. Many of them wished us well and hoped that we would win the Olympics thus doing them honor. Those who came in behind us at Orchard Beach could always say they rowed against the best in the world, that they were a part of the Olympic victory. They pushed us and we rowed for them as well as for country, club and city.

Our 1964 crew dismissed the myth sustained by so many successful college coaches that an Olympic crew had to come from their ranks, that only in the college environment could the necessary cohesiveness be attained. Our Vesper group was cohesive, of single purpose once in the boat and rowing All Together, even though a stranger might not know so in hearing our bickering conversations on shore. We came from different backgrounds and did not have that much in common beyond an oar.

To my surprise I subsequently learned that the preceding Olympic champion, the Ratzeburg eight that won at Rome in 1960, was similar to Vesper in this aspect. After Rome those oarsmen never held a reunion, seldom if ever saw one another again, according to writings by professor Hans Lenk of the Technical University of Berlin. Hans Lenk rowed in that crew and was close to the coach, Karl Adam.

Dr. William P. Morgan, the director of the exercise psychology laboratory at the University of Wisconsin in Madison, endorsed the findings of Professor Lenk in finding that a personal cohesiveness is not necessary for mature athletes competing at the highest levels. We in the Vesper crew demonstrated that All Together in the boat was enough.

Ours was a one shot deal and the successful combination would not have endured forever. Boyce Budd summed it up when he said, "We would have had a mass brawl if we had to survive another couple of years together. We were so extraordinarily lucky in so many ways, the timing and the chemistry, a hundred factors.

"And so I just find myself pinching myself and saying. 'Man oh man, are you a lucky dude.' It came together and we showed just how hard it is to pull off this sort of thing."

I cannot believe that there ever was a crew quite like ours and I know that there has not been one since.

Both Tom Amlong and Emory Clark retired after Tokyo, but the rest of us rowed in 1965. At Henley, we set a new course record of 6:18 in beating another undefeated Harvard crew. Two days later, we repeated the record time, but a new Ratzeburg crew reset the record, defeating us while rowing a 6:16. Invited to Germany the next week, we raced on the Ratzeburg home course and lost in a photo finish. Further watered down, we embarked in the spring of 1966 on a State Department Goodwill Tour of Egypt and the Balkans, rowing at Henley en route home.

Vesper was never again able to duplicate or exceed the effort put forth on the 15th of October, 1964, when they truly had it ALL TOGETHER.

36

Where Are the Medals Now?

Many years have passed. It took forty years before another American eight-oared men's crew could again win Olympic gold medals.

Much has changed as to equipment and organization. Carbon fibers have replaced wood, both in the boats and the oars. Indubitably the shells are stronger, lighter, faster. The National Association of Amateur Oarsmen became the United States Rowing Association, a more befitting name because of the many women now in the sport and because the word amateur no longer had much utility. The amateur code with all its rules has disappeared. Many countries, the U.S. included, reward their Olympic medal winners with cash prizes. Hence, our Vesper crew will forever be the last American amateur eight to win the Olympics.

The Olympic format has changed. Racing for the pair-with-coxswain and the four-with-coxswain has been eliminated to make room for the women crews and the lightweights, meaning crews whose average weight cannot exceed a certain standard.

Coaches from abroad have come to the U.S. with promises to restore America's rowing predominance and millions of dollars have been spent on development, training and equipment. But not until 2004, when the U.S. men's eight won at Athens, was the American entry able to match the achievement of the rag-tag Vesper bunch.

Our gold medals were cast by the Japanese government mint and they contained only about five dollars worth of actual gold plate. I was once offered $5,000 for mine, at a collectors' memorabilia show in Lake Placid, N.Y., where I now live. I didn't bite. As it affirms the personal status of "best in the world" the medal is of greater value to me than five thousand dollars or any amount of dollars.

What has happened to the medals that were draped around our necks in the dark October 15, 1964?

Bowman Joe Amlong has his medal hidden in his pantry in his Vero Beach, Florida, home. Joe's marriage to Gail, which upset brother Tom, has been a been a good and strong one and together they brought up two wonderful daughters. Joe spent 20 years on active duty in the Air Force and after retirement he enjoyed the wild west in Grand Cole, Montana, before heading to Florida.

The years have taken their toll on this feisty and outspoken Amlong brother who overcame cancer recently. My time with Joe and Gail researching information for this book was most pleasant. He's mellowed since Tokyo.

◆   ◆   ◆

After a few years as head coach of rowing at Boston University, Hugh Foley became a financial advisor and now lives in Eugene, Oregon. Hugh writes, "My medal sat in a box with other memorabilia, newspaper clippings, etc., for many years. I'd haul it out every four years to show someone writing a local interest story during an Olympic year or to show visitors and friends. My wife and children thought it should be left on the coffee table for everyone to enjoy. As late as 1996 I still had the lacquer box and ribbon.

"In June,1996, our house was robbed. They took all the small items that could be thrown in a pillow case, my wife's jewelry (some of it heirloom stuff), a coin collection, a dozen trading pins, and my gold medal.

"We reported the theft to the police and they were marginally helpful even though our heist was pretty small potatoes. One detective decided he would do everything possible to try and find the medal. We talked every day for two to three weeks with no tangible results. However, he felt he had an idea of who was fencing the loot and figured out some way to put the squeeze on the guy.

"Out of the blue the detective called one day to say he'd found my medal. When I got it back the beautiful black lacquered box and the ribbon were gone. What he handed me was recognizable as Olympic gold but the banditos had nipped it, gouged it, scratched it and bitten it to see if it was solid gold.

"I've still got the medal. It's in a sock drawer in the dresser and it looks like it fell off the bus at freeway speed. Every four years at Olympic time I haul it out for show and tell."

◆   ◆   ◆

Stan Cwiklinski, our three man, retired as a commander in the Navy after a full career in underwater salvage operations. His Naval Officer wife is still on active duty in California. His daughter Stacia graduated from the U.S. Coast Guard Academy and is serving on active duty. Stan is rebuilding his retirement home in Hampton, Virginia, and wrote, "My medal resides in a narrow, gold painted, wooden shadow box and hangs proudly on my living room wall.

"Up to about 15 years ago, it accompanied me everywhere I traveled throughout my Navy career in its silk lined, black lacquered wood presentation box. Except when I showed it off, it was far from view, squirreled away inside an old, white cotton sweat sock. During my deployments to South Vietnam, my parents took care of it, hiding it in its box on the floor of their bedroom closet inside a shoe container with a bunch of my small bits and pieces of memorabilia. There it miraculously survived a burglary. My wife Lisa and I will bequeath the medal to our daughter Stacia."

◆　　　◆　　　◆

Tom Amlong, a retired Army captain, lives in Old Lyme, Connecticut, with his wife and daughters. Like Joe's, Tom's career in the military was stalled by the rowing and he did not advance in rank after the games. Tom's medal is hidden in his home, away from possible thieves who would have to wade through press clippings, rowing programs, pictures, and other remnants of a life devoted to rowing. Tom's latest fight is against cancer attributed to agent orange from a Vietnam deployment.

Tom made an effort to assist with the local high school rowing program but found that the politics were not to his liking. Perhaps his rough attitude did not help when instructing 14-year old girls in how to pull an oar. When he visited the Coast Guard Academy boat house where I was coaching in 1981, I had to ask him to leave after he held an impromptu clinic with my oarsmen, saying that I was not coaching them properly.

As voted by the remaining members of the Vesper crew, Tom was chosen as the more obnoxious of the two brothers. In an effort to best describe Tom, I resorted to my Roget's Thesaurus and found 71 adjectives ranging from outrageous to wretched. One word that did not fit was worthless, because Tom was of great value when it came to pulling his weight and being a muscle part of the All Together effort.

Tom also has mellowed. As we walked his dog in the woods of Old Lyme one day he explained his theory in 1964. He claimed that he acted the way he did to bring out the anger and the best in his teammates. He had no apology for his unpleasant nature but requested that I understand and go easy on him while writing the account of the events leading up to our victory in Tokyo. According to Tom, it was just an act to help us to victory. All these years I thought Tom was naturally obnoxious. Sorry about that.

◆   ◆   ◆

Emory Clark lives in Metamora, Michigan, where he practices law. He and his wife Christina have a daughter, Lucy. A sportsman and fisherman, Clark travels to trout and salmon streams from Scotland to New Zealand. He still rows and recently won a gold medal at the Masters World championships in Montreal in a four with Dietrich Rose, John Higginson, and Ted Nash.

He reports, "My medal is usually in the dresser drawer with the socks and the underwear where it has been for the last 40 years. Once the medal made it home across the Pacific, it traveled extensively to athletic dinners, schools and colleges, rowing banquets and service club meetings as every four years someone remembers I was an Olympian.

"It spent a month or more in a local library exhibit and has been on display in the hardware store and gas station of my home town of Metamora. It has gone home with lots of folks who needed to show it to their kids or neighbors. It has been touched by thousands of hands and has been photographed around the necks of many. The hinge on its lovely black lacquered box is broken and its multicolored ribbon is less than pristine from all the eager fingers. But the medal itself still embodies the spirit of the Games, untarnished by the commercialism, the drugs, the cheating and pretension that seem to characterize much of today's Olympics."

◆   ◆   ◆

Boyce Budd's home in Devon, Pennsylvania, was burglarized in the spring of 1980 and the medal was stolen and never recovered. According to Boyce, "The medal had been displayed at an art museum with my name and address on it and it is possible that the thieves got the idea from that although I doubt that criminals patronize art exhibits. In any event other of my less important medals were recovered from a stream bed in the Poconos when the crooks realized that they did not have any value. But the gold token of greatness from the Games was never discovered."

Budd asked the U.S. Olympic committee about a replacement and someone queried the Japanese. But the die from whence the medal was struck had been destroyed intentionally to prevent phony duplicates. That was that, a tragic loss.

Canadian John Lecky, Budd's bowman at Cambridge University and at Henley, and Clark got together and asked a mutual friend, a jeweler in Montreal, to try to cast a duplicate of Emory's medal as a surprise gift for Boyce. That worked and the replica cannot be distinguished from the original. Boyce hides it in a dark closet in the box in which it was presented to him by his friends.

Budd had a successful career with several air freight companies and resides with his wife on a small farm in Bucks County where he is active in politics. He has stated in his will that his two sons will share the medal, rotating possession every three years. According to Budd, "Friends joke that I wear it around my neck at all times, which is untrue. We simply don't talk much about the medal, only the victory in Japan."

Coach Allen Rosenberg, Bob Zimonyi, Boyce Budd, Bill Knecht and Bill Stowe receiving awards from Pfizer after returning to the United States.

Bill Knecht wears his medal, and it resides around his neck in the Calvary Cemetery in Cherry Hill, New Jersey, where Bill is buried next to his son, Teddy. Bill died of cancer after a solid career in the sheet metal contracting business, and after serving the rowing sport so ably in numerous elected positions of responsibility. His widow Joan made the decision to bury Bill with the medal, avoiding a decision within his large family as to who would have possession.

Bill's grandson, Kevin Knecht, wore his grandfather's Olympic racing shirt under his team jersey when he was coxing crews, first in high school and then at Marietta College in Ohio.

In researching for this book I discovered Bill had suffered from hereditary manic depression which he self medicated with rowing, his work, wine and women. Bill was always on the go, either rowing or handling his million dollar business. According to Joan, he would come home exhausted in the evening and they shared a bottle of wine before he consumed his normal pint of vanilla ice cream.

Bill and Joan were divorced after she discovered that Bill had fathered two children by Ana Tomas, a former Rumanian sculler who was brought to the United States by Jack Kelly. She died of cancer one year before Bill was stricken with the same disease. Bill and Joan were remarried a week before he died.

◆   ◆   ◆

My own gold medal was taken away for safe keeping by my mother when a bartender at a local Bronxville tavern called to say that I had left it on the bar. The medal was a great means to free beer. When I had matured sufficiently to satisfy Mom, she returned it and since then it has done the tour of dinners, meetings, and various show and tell opportunities.

I feel that the medal does not belong to me alone, but that it belongs also to the United States and I am happy to share it with the nation that offered me the opportunity to participate in the Olympic games. It has been auctioned off at several charity events, the winner earning the right to wear it for the evening.

When I was coaching at the Coast Guard Academy, and the budget would not meet the crew program's needs, I publicly announced that I would auction off the medal to raise money for a new shell. The embarrassed administration found the necessary funds and I was told not to pull that stunt again.

For the past six years it has been set up on a table along the route of the Lake Placid running course for 1,700 Ironman contestants to touch for good luck near the end of the 140-mile ordeal.

One time I was driving to New York, where I was to visit two Brooklyn grade school assemblies in conjunction with the city's campaign to host the 2012 Olympics. A State Trooper stopped me for speeding. I was running late and had 200 miles to go. The trooper could see I was alert, dressed in a fresh shirt and tie, and when I explained what I was doing and pulled the medal from my pocket, he promptly dismissed me. "Well, you had better get going," he said. The medal got me out of a speeding ticket.

I have bequeathed my medal to the Vesper Boat Club, where hopefully it will hang to inspire future generations of oarsmen and women.

◆　　　◆　　　◆

Our coxswain, Bob Zimonyi, kept his medal in a safe deposit box at his bank in Miami Beach. Bob retired from his position with the Sandmeyer Steel Company and moved to Florida for health reasons some years ago. He had heart problems and died in January, 2004, at the age of 87.

He was living with his companion of over 45 years, Isabel Gressner, a lovely lady with a Spanish-Cuban background. While he lived one block from the Ronald W. Shane Watersports Center in Miami Beach he was never seen hanging around the boat house. Robby retired from coxing in the late 1960's and never looked back. He knew when it was time to leave the party and he left a legacy difficult to match.

◆　　　◆　　　◆

Jack Kelly was not awarded a medal, but took immense pride in the Vesper accomplishment and it eased his failure to personally win the coveted prize during his competitive career. He had been elected Chairman of the United States Olympic Committee when he died of heart failure in 1985 while jogging home from a rowing workout on the Schuylkill River.

◆　　　◆　　　◆

Dietrich Rose, also went medal-less but continued to assist with the Vesper program for years. He continues to row with the Masters program and races internationally. He is President/Owner of a successful engineering firm in Philadelphia.

◆   ◆   ◆

Allen Rosenberg, a practicing patent law attorney and a part time rowing coach in Washington, D.C., still complains that coaches are not awarded medals and if he had one he says he would never tell me where it is....

Bow to stern, left to right, top row: Bowman Joe Amlong, Hugh Foley, Stan Cwiklinski, Tom Amlong, Emory Clark, Boyce Budd, Bill Knecht, and stroke Bill Stowe. Coxswain Bob Zimonyi is in the middle between the big guys.

Index

0-595-34388-0

Made in the USA
Lexington, KY
16 January 2014